RAYSHAUN "CHU" SMITH

Breaking The Code: Thriving as Black Individuals in the Era of Artificial Intelligence

Contents

Preface

In recent years, artificial intelligence (AI) has become an inescapable force, touching every aspect of our lives. From the applications we use daily to the systems that drive our economy, AI has redefined the way we interact with the world around us. As an independent researcher and AI/Tech enthusiast with a deep interest in the societal implications of AI, I have observed the challenges and opportunities that this new era of intelligence presents, particularly for Black individuals navigating this ever-evolving landscape.

The inspiration for "Breaking the Code: Thriving as Black Individuals in the Era of Artificial Intelligence" emerged from my experiences, conversations, and observations, coupled with a desire to provide a comprehensive and accessible guide for those seeking to better understand the unique position of Black individuals in the AI-driven world. This book aims to bridge the gap between the technical aspects of AI and the real-world consequences of its deployment, equipping readers with the necessary knowledge to advocate for a more equitable and just future.

Throughout this book, I will take you on a journey that starts with the basics of AI and its history, delving into the inner workings of machine learning algorithms and neural networks. We will explore the various types of AI systems and their applications, illuminating the real-world impact of this groundbreaking technology. Along the way, we will examine the often-overlooked issue of algorithmic discrimination and the historical exclusion of Black communities from the technological sphere. Together, we will navigate the ethical and societal implications of AI, seeking meaningful transparency and redress for the harms that may arise from its use.

As we embark on this journey, it is crucial to remember that "Breaking the Code" is not merely a technical guide or historical account; it is also a call to action. This book is a manifesto for change, urging readers to advocate for a more inclusive and just AI landscape that respects the rights, dignity, and agency of all individuals, especially those from underrepresented and marginalized communities. While I wrote this book specifically to address the experiences of Black individuals, the insights and lessons offered are applicable to everyone who seeks to create a more equitable future. By understanding the complexities of AI and its implications, we can collectively work towards creating a future where technology serves as a force for good, empowering all members of society.

So, as you turn the pages of "Breaking the Code," I invite you to join me in the pursuit of knowledge and the quest for a more equitable world, where all individuals can thrive in the era of AI. Together, we can forge a path towards a brighter, more inclusive future for all.

-Rayshaun "Chu" Smith

Acknowledgement

Thanks to my family for their incredible support. Thanks also to Brandon Bivens, Melanie Smith, Kary Flint, Cory Miller, and Cierra Strange. Thanks to Cathy O'Neil, Dr. Safiya Umoja, Ruha Benjamin, and Dr Joy Buolamwini whom lifetime work serves as my inspiration. Thanks to all the people without whom this book would not exist; everyone who planted the seed by telling me after engaging in casual conversations that I should write a book, my genuine supporters, anyone who has slandered me - you threw dirt on my name and flowers grew. Finally, I would like to express my deepest gratitude to those who have tirelessly warned about the potential dangers of AI for years, specifically women and women of color. These trailblazers have been at the forefront of highlighting the harm that automated decision-making can cause, particularly to marginalized communities. Their research, contributions, courage, and strength have been instrumental in shaping our understanding of AI and its implications on society. I am deeply thankful for their unwavering commitment to advocating for a more inclusive and equitable future in the realm of AI. To all the women and women of color who have dedicated their lives to this cause, we celebrate your resilience and impact, and we honor the critical role you play in creating a better world for everyone.

1

The Dawn of Intelligent Machines: Setting the Stage for AI and Its Impact on Black Communities

In this chapter, we will introduce AI and discuss its significance for society, particularly for Black individuals who often face unique challenges in the age of intelligent machines.

AI is a multidisciplinary field that encompasses various branches of computer science, mathematics, and engineering. The primary goal of AI is to create intelligent agents or systems capable of learning, reasoning, problem-solving, and adapting to complex environments. AI has the potential to transform industries, improve the lives of individuals worldwide, and accelerate the pace of human progress.

For Black communities, AI presents both opportunities and challenges. On one hand, it offers the potential for social and economic advancement by providing access to resources, tools, and information that were previously out of reach. AI-powered educational platforms can help bridge the digital divide and offer personalized learning experiences for students from underserved backgrounds. Similarly, AI-driven healthcare applications can improve the diagnosis and treatment of diseases that disproportionately affect Black individuals, such as sickle cell anemia or hypertension.

However, AI systems can also reinforce and perpetuate existing biases and inequalities. For instance, AI algorithms used in hiring and lending processes have been found to discriminate against Black applicants, restricting their access to jobs and financial resources. In the realm of criminal justice, AI-driven tools facial recognition technology and predictive policing algorithms can intensify the over-policing of Black communities and reinforce racial profiling.

In light of these potential consequences, it is essential for Black individuals to understand the intricacies of AI systems and actively participate in shaping the development and deployment of this technology. By engaging in conversations about AI ethics, transparency, and accountability, we can work towards ensuring that AI is used as a tool for empowerment and equity, rather than a mechanism for further marginalization.

1.1 The Origins of AI

The history of AI can be traced back to ancient civilizations, where myths and stories about artificial beings endowed with human-like intelligence and abilities were common. While the modern concept of AI emerged in the mid-20th century, it was mathematician and logician Alan Turing who laid the foundation for computer science and theoretical AI with his groundbreaking work on computation and machine intelligence. Turing's ideas set the stage for the development of electronic computers and sparked the first wave of AI research, which primarily focused on rule-based systems and symbolic representations of knowledge.

Over the next few decades, AI research expanded to include new methods and techniques, such as artificial neural networks, which sought to mimic the structure and function of the human brain. These early AI systems, known as "connectionist" models, demonstrated the potential for learning and adaptation, but they were limited in their ability to handle complex tasks and large-scale problems.

In the late 1990s and early 2000s, AI research experienced a resurgence, fueled by the increasing availability of computational power and the advent of the internet, which provided access to vast amounts of data. This period saw the development of machine learning algorithms capable of processing and learning from large datasets, as well as the emergence of deep learning, a subset of machine learning that focuses on the development of artificial neural networks with multiple layers. These advancements have enabled AI systems to tackle increasingly complex tasks, such as natural language processing, image recognition, and autonomous decision-making.

1.2 The Impact of AI on Black Communities: Opportunities and Challenges

As AI systems have become more sophisticated and pervasive, their impact on society has grown, with profound implications for Black communities. In this section, we will explore some of the key opportunities and challenges that AI presents for Black individuals, as well as potential strategies for addressing these issues.

Education

AI-driven educational tools have the potential to revolutionize learning by providing personalized, adaptive instruction that caters to the unique needs and abilities of each student. For Black students, who often face systemic barriers to educational success, such as under funded schools and limited access to advanced courses, AI-powered platforms can offer a means to bridge the gap and level the playing field.

Healthcare

AI has shown great promise in revolutionizing healthcare by improving the diagnosis and treatment of diseases, optimizing resource allocation, and facilitating personalized medicine. For Black individuals, who often experience disparities in healthcare access and outcomes, AI-driven healthcare applications can help address these challenges by improving the accuracy and efficiency of medical decision-making, enhancing patient-provider communication, and reducing health disparities.

Economic Opportunity

AI has the potential to reshape labor markets and create new economic opportunities for Black individuals. By automating repetitive tasks and augmenting human capabilities, AI can enable workers to focus on higher-value activities, leading to increased productivity and economic growth.

The rise of AI also poses risks for job displacement, particularly for workers in low-skilled occupations, which may disproportionately affect Black communities. To mitigate these risks, it is essential to invest in education and workforce development programs that prepare Black individuals for the jobs of the future and equip them with the skills necessary to succeed in the AI-driven economy.

Criminal Justice

As previously mentioned, AI-powered tools such as facial recognition technology and predictive policing algorithms have been increasingly adopted by law enforcement agencies, raising concerns about their potential impact on civil liberties and racial bias. To address these concerns, it is crucial to advocate for greater transparency, accountability, and oversight in the development and deployment of AI tools in the criminal justice system, as well as to push for the prohibition of certain uses of AI that threaten civil liberties and disproportionately harm Black communities.

1.3 Advocating for a More Equitable AI Future

As we navigate the era of AI, it is essential for Black individuals to play an active role in shaping the development and deployment of AI systems. This involves engaging in conversations about AI ethics, transparency, and accountability, and advocating for policies and practices that promote equitable AI. By doing so, we can help ensure that AI serves as a force for empowerment and social progress, rather than a tool for further marginalization.

1.4 Key Organizations in AI

As AI continues to advance, numerous organizations are playing pivotal roles in shaping the future of this technology. These organizations range from academic institutions and research centers to private companies and government agencies, each contributing their expertise and resources to the development and deployment of AI systems. In the context of advocating for a more equitable AI future, it is important for Black individuals to be aware of these organizations and engage with them, as they wield significant influence over the direction of AI research and development.

Some key organizations involved in AI include major technology companies, academic institutions and research centers, non-profit organizations and advocacy groups, and government agencies and intergovernmental organizations. By engaging with these organizations and participating in their initiatives, Black individuals can help shape the development and deployment of AI in ways that promote equity, fairness, and social justice.

The era of AI has arrived, bringing with it a myriad of opportunities and challenges for society as a whole, and for Black communities in particular. As we continue to explore the intricacies of AI and its impact on our lives, it is crucial for Black individuals to be active participants in this rapidly evolving landscape. By understanding the history, fundamentals, and ethical implications of AI, and by advocating for a more equitable AI future, we can help ensure that this powerful technology serves as a force for good and a tool for empowerment, rather than a mechanism for further marginalization.

In the following chapters of "Breaking the Code: Thriving as Black Individuals in the Era of Artificial Intelligence," we will dive even deeper into the topics outlined in this first chapter, providing readers with the knowledge and resources necessary to navigate the age of AI with confidence and resilience.

2

Unraveling the AI Labyrinth: Key Concepts and Terminologies

As we delve further into the world of AI, it is essential to familiarize ourselves with the key concepts and terminologies that will help us navigate this exciting and complex field. In this chapter, we will break down some of the most important terms and concepts that you will encounter throughout this book, providing a solid foundation for understanding the nuances of AI and its implications for Black communities.

Artificial Intelligence (AI)

AI refers to the development of computer systems capable of performing tasks that would normally require human intelligence, such as visual perception, speech recognition, decision-making, and natural language understanding. The term "artificial intelligence" is often used to describe any machine or system that exhibits traits associated with a human mind, such as learning and problem-solving.

Machine Learning (ML)

Machine learning is a subfield of AI that focuses on the development of algorithms that can learn patterns and make decisions based on data, rather than relying on explicit programming. In other words, machine learning enables computers to learn from experience and improve their performance over time. There are various types of machine learning, including supervised learning, unsupervised learning, and reinforcement learning, each with its unique approach to learning from data.

Deep Learning (DL)

Deep learning is a specialized form of machine learning that uses artificial neural networks to model complex patterns in data. Inspired by the structure and function of the human brain, deep learning algorithms consist of layers of interconnected nodes (neurons) that process and transmit information. Deep learning has been particularly successful in tasks such as image and speech recognition, natural language processing, and playing complex games like Go and chess.

Neural Networks

Neural networks are a type of machine learning model that is designed to mimic the way the human brain processes information. They consist of interconnected nodes or neurons, which are organized into layers. Each neuron receives input from other neurons, processes that input, and then passes its output to other neurons in the network. Neural networks can be trained to recognize patterns in data and make predictions or decisions based on those patterns.

Algorithm

An algorithm is a set of instructions or rules that a computer follows to solve a problem or perform a task. In the context of AI and machine learning, algorithms are used to process data, learn patterns, and make decisions based on that data. Some common machine learning algorithms include decision trees, support vector machines, and deep learning models like convolutional neural networks.

Data

Data is the foundation of AI and machine learning. It refers to the information that is used to train, validate, and test machine learning models. Data can come in various forms, such as text, images, audio, and video, and can be structured (organized into a specific format) or unstructured (not organized in a predefined format). In order to develop effective AI systems, large amounts of high-quality data are often required, as the quality and quantity of data can directly impact the performance of the AI system.

Training and Testing

In the context of machine learning, training refers to the process of teaching a model to recognize patterns in data and make decisions based on those patterns. This is typically achieved by feeding the model a large dataset (called the training set), which consists of input-output pairs that the model can learn from. Once the model has been trained, it can then be tested on a separate dataset (called the testing set) to evaluate its performance and generalizability to new, unseen data.

Bias

Bias in AI and machine learning refers to the presence of systematic errors in a model's predictions, often resulting from flawed or unrepresentative training data. Bias can lead to unfair and discriminatory outcomes, particularly when AI systems are used in sensitive areas such as hiring, lending, and policing. Addressing bias in AI is crucial in order to create equitable and just systems that serve the needs of all individuals, including those from marginalized and underrepresented communities.

Algorithmic Discrimination

Algorithmic discrimination occurs when an AI system's decisions or recommendations unfairly disadvantage a particular group of people based on their race, gender, age, or other protected characteristics. This can happen when biased data is used to train the AI system or when the algorithm itself is designed in a way that perpetuates or amplifies existing inequalities. Combating algorithmic discrimination is vital to ensure that AI systems are fair and equitable for all users, particularly for Black individuals who have historically been subjected to various forms of discrimination.

Natural Language Processing (NLP)

Natural language processing is a subfield of AI that focuses on the interaction between computers and human language. NLP systems are designed to understand, interpret, and generate human language in a way that is both meaningful and useful. Some common NLP tasks include sentiment analysis, machine translation, and question-answering systems. NLP has significant implications for creating more accessible and inclusive AI systems that can understand and respond to the diverse linguistic and cultural needs of users.

Computer Vision

Computer vision is another subfield of AI that focuses on enabling computers to interpret and understand visual information from the world. This includes tasks such as object recognition, facial recognition, and scene understanding. Computer vision has numerous applications, from self-driving cars to medical imaging, but it also raises concerns about privacy, surveillance, and the potential for biased or discriminatory outcomes in systems that rely on facial recognition or other visual data.

Reinforcement Learning

Reinforcement learning is a type of machine learning in which an AI system learns to make decisions by interacting with its environment and receiving feedback in the form of rewards or penalties. The goal of reinforcement learning is for the AI system to learn an optimal policy or strategy for making decisions that maximize the cumulative reward over time. Reinforcement learning has been used to train AI systems to play complex games like Go and chess, as well as to control robots and autonomous vehicles.

Ethics and AI

As AI systems become more advanced and integrated into various aspects of society, questions around the ethical implications of AI are becoming increasingly important. This includes issues such as privacy, surveillance, fairness, accountability, and the potential for AI systems can perpetuate or worsen existing social inequalities. It is essential for researchers, policymakers, and industry leaders to consider these ethical dimensions when developing and deploying AI technologies, particularly in contexts where the potential for harm is significant.

In this chapter, we have introduced some of the key concepts and terminologies that will help you better understand the world of AI and its impact on Black communities. With this foundation in place, we will now explore the history of AI, its development, and the organizations shaping its future in the next chapters.

3

Tracing the Digital Footsteps: The Evolution of AI Through History

The development of AI has been a gradual process spanning several decades, with roots in various fields such as mathematics, philosophy, computer science, and cognitive psychology. This chapter will provide an overview of the key milestones in AI's evolution and their implications for Black communities.

In ancient times, thinkers like Aristotle and the Chinese philosopher Mozi pondered the nature of intelligence and the potential for creating artificial minds. These early ideas laid the groundwork for the birth of modern AI. As we mentioned in Chapter 1, the foundations of AI were established in the early 20th century, with key contributions from Alan Turing, who laid the groundwork for computer science and conceived the idea of a universal machine. Building upon the insights shared in the first chapter, let's dive deeper into how the field of AI has evolved over time, exploring the different approaches and innovations that have shaped its growth and development. By understanding the historical context and milestones in AI research, we can better appreciate the progress made and the challenges that still lie ahead.

In 1950, Turing published his seminal paper "Computing Machinery and Intelligence," proposing what is now known as the Turing Test – a criterion for determining whether a machine exhibits intelligent behavior indistinguishable from that of a human. The same year, American mathematician Claude Shannon published his influential paper "Programming a Computer for Playing Chess," which discussed the development of an algorithm for playing chess and demonstrated that computers could be programmed to perform complex tasks, paving the way for AI research.

The 1950s and 1960s saw a surge of interest in AI, fueled by optimism about the potential for machines to replicate human intelligence. In 1956, the Dartmouth Conference, organized by AI pioneers John McCarthy, Marvin Minsky, Nathaniel Rochester, and Claude Shannon, marked the official birth of AI as an academic discipline. During this period, researchers developed early AI programs like Samuel's checkers-playing program, Newell and Simon's Logic Theorist, and McCarthy's Lisp programming language, which became the dominant language for AI programming.

At the same time, the field of AI began to diverge into several subfields, each focused on different aspects of intelligence. Some researchers pursued symbolic AI, which sought to replicate human reasoning and problem-solving using formal logic and rule-based systems. Others explored connectionism, an approach inspired by the structure and functioning of the human brain, which led to the development of early neural networks. These varied approaches, while often competing, contributed to the growth and diversification of AI research.

During the 1960s and 1970s, AI research received significant funding from governments and private industry, driven by the belief that human-level AI was within reach. This period saw the development of influential AI systems like SHRDLU, a natural language processing system that could manipulate virtual objects in a simple block world, and MYCIN, an expert system designed to diagnose and recommend treatments for bacterial infections. These early successes sparked excitement and further investment in AI research.

As we move through the history of AI, it's important to note that the late 1970s and early 1980s marked a challenging period for the field, characterized by reduced funding and disillusionment, now referred to as the "AI winter." During this time, many AI researchers adjusted their goals from pursuing human-level intelligence to concentrating on more specialized, narrow AI applications, targeting specific tasks like speech recognition, computer vision, and expert systems for various industries.

The 1980s also saw the emergence of new AI approaches, such as knowledge-based systems, which relied on large databases of domain-specific information, and machine learning, which focused on developing algorithms that could learn and improve over time. These developments, along with advances in computer hardware and processing power, led to a resurgence of interest in AI research and development in the late 1980s and 1990s. During this period, AI began to be integrated into various sectors, including finance, healthcare, manufacturing, and telecommunications, demonstrating its potential for widespread practical applications.

The 1990s also marked the rise of the World Wide Web, which dramatically increased the availability of digital data and provided a rich resource for AI researchers to develop and refine machine learning algorithms. This period saw significant advancements in natural language processing, enabling AI systems to better understand and interact with human language, as well as in computer vision, allowing machines to perceive and interpret images more accurately.

In the early 2000s, the field of AI experienced another major breakthrough with the development of deep learning, a subfield of machine learning that focuses on training artificial neural networks with multiple layers. Deep learning techniques, combined with the increasing availability of powerful computing hardware and large datasets, led to significant improvements in AI performance across a range of tasks, including image and speech recognition, natural language understanding, and game playing.

AI's rapid progress during this period led to growing concerns about its potential impact on society, particularly for marginalized and vulnerable communities. In particular, the increasing use of AI in decision-making processes across various sectors raised questions about the fairness and transparency of these systems, as well as their potential to perpetuate existing biases and inequalities.

For Black communities, the rise of AI has presented both opportunities and challenges. On one hand, AI technologies have the potential to revolutionize industries and create new economic opportunities, which could benefit historically disadvantaged communities. AI-powered tools can also help address long-standing social issues. On the other hand research has revealed that AI algorithms can adopt and propagate societal biases found in the training data. In addition, the growing reliance on AI in surveillance technologies has sparked worries about the possibility of extensive surveillance and the diminishing of privacy rights, especially for marginalized communities that have historically faced imbalanced surveillance and policing.

Examining the key milestones in AI's development, we can better appreciate its potential and its limitations, and work towards harnessing its power for the benefit of all members of society. As AI continued to advance in the 2010s, it began to permeate nearly every aspect of our daily lives, transforming industries and reshaping the way we interact with technology. This era saw the emergence of virtual personal assistants like Siri and Alexa, as well as the widespread adoption of AI-powered recommendation systems in e-commerce, music, and video streaming services. Self-driving cars, once a futuristic concept, started to become a reality, thanks to advances in AI-driven computer vision and sensor technologies.

During this period, AI research also saw remarkable progress in the field of reinforcement learning, a type of machine learning in which an agent learns to make decisions by interacting with its environment and receiving feedback in the form of rewards or penalties. The success of reinforcement learning techniques was demonstrated by AI systems such as AlphaGo, developed by DeepMind, which defeated world champion Go players in 2016, and OpenAI's Dota 2-playing AI, which triumphed over professional gamers in 2018.

While these successes highlighted the immense potential of AI, they also brought to the forefront the ethical and societal implications of the technology. The increasing integration of AI in various decision-making processes led to a growing awareness of the potential for algorithmic bias, which can result in discriminatory outcomes for marginalized communities, including Black individuals. For instance, biased facial recognition systems have been shown to disproportionately misidentify Black people, which can have severe consequences when used in law enforcement or security settings.

As awareness of these issues grew, a new field of AI research known as "fairness, accountability, and transparency in machine learning" (FAT-ML) emerged, aiming to develop methods to measure and mitigate biases in AI systems. This interdisciplinary field brings together researchers from computer science, social sciences, and humanities to address the ethical and societal challenges posed by AI, with a focus on developing more equitable and accountable AI technologies.

The recognition of these challenges has also led to increased calls for greater diversity and representation within the AI research community, which has historically been dominated by individuals from predominantly White and male backgrounds. Increasing diversity in AI research can help ensure that the perspectives and concerns of underrepresented communities, including Black individuals, are adequately considered in the design and development of AI systems.

As we continue to trace the evolution of AI through history, it is crucial to recognize the potential risks and challenges it poses, particularly for marginalized communities, and to work towards developing AI technologies that are equitable, accountable, and aligned with our shared values and aspirations. In the current era, we are witnessing AI's rapid growth and widespread adoption across various sectors, with its ethical and social implications becoming increasingly prominent. Governments, businesses, and civil society organizations are now grappling with the challenge of governing AI technologies to maximize their benefits while minimizing potential harms, particularly for marginalized communities such as Black individuals.

As AI systems become more sophisticated, they are beginning to demonstrate capabilities that were once thought to be the exclusive domain of human intelligence. For example, AI-powered language models like OpenAI's GPT series can generate human-like text, opening new possibilities for applications such as translation, summarization, and content generation. In the field of computer vision, AI systems can now recognize and categorize objects, scenes, and people with remarkable accuracy, enabling advances in areas like autonomous vehicles and medical imaging.

As we previously discussed, the ongoing development of AI technologies brings about emerging ethical and societal challenges. The incorporation of AI into decision-making areas, such as recruitment, financing, and medical assessments, raises concerns about transparency, fairness, and responsibility. Furthermore, the growing reliance on AI in surveillance tools, like facial recognition systems, introduces potential risks to privacy and civil rights, particularly for vulnerable populations with a history of excessive policing and prejudice.t.

To address these concerns, researchers, policymakers, and activists are exploring various approaches, including developing technical methods to measure and mitigate biases in AI systems, advocating for legal and regulatory frameworks to govern the use of AI, and promoting transparency and public engagement in AI development and deployment processes.

One notable example is the work of the Algorithmic Justice League, an organization founded by Joy Buolamwini, which aims to create a more equitable and accountable AI ecosystem through research, policy guidance, and media advocacy. By raising awareness of the potential harms and biases of AI systems and empowering communities to hold decision-makers accountable, the Algorithmic Justice League and similar organizations are playing a vital role in shaping the future of AI in a more just and inclusive direction.

As we reflect on the evolution of AI through history, it is essential to recognize that the development and deployment of AI technologies are not merely technical challenges but also fundamentally social and political endeavors. By understanding the historical context of AI and engaging with its ethical and societal implications, we can work towards a future where AI serves the needs and aspirations of all people, including Black individuals, fostering greater equity, justice, and empowerment.

In this chapter, we traced the digital footsteps of AI, journeying through its fascinating history and exploring the significant milestones that have shaped its development. From its early beginnings in the realm of philosophy to the breakthroughs of the 20th and 21st centuries, we have seen how AI has evolved to become an integral part of our modern world. We delved into the works of visionaries like Alan Turing, John McCarthy, and Marvin Minsky, who laid the foundations for AI's growth, and examined how the field has progressed through various stages of optimism, skepticism, and resurgence.

As we concluded this chapter, we gained a deeper appreciation for the rich tapestry of AI's past, which serves as the backdrop for the current advancements and challenges we face today. Armed with this historical context, we are better equipped to understand the complexities of AI and its potential implications for society, especially for Black individuals and other underrepresented communities.

4

Powerhouses of AI: Organizations Shaping the AI Landscape

In this chapter, we explore the most influential organizations shaping the AI landscape and their contributions to the field, as well as discuss the potential effects of their work on the Black community. These organizations can be categorized into three main groups: private companies, academic and research institutions, and non-profit and advocacy organizations.

1.1 Private Companies Google (DeepMind and Google Brain)

Google, a multinational technology giant, plays a major role in AI research and development through its two main research arms: DeepMind and Google Brain. DeepMind, a London-based AI company acquired by Google in 2014, focuses on artificial general intelligence (AGI) and has been behind several breakthroughs in AI. Google Brain, based in Mountain View, California, is dedicated to advancing AI through deep learning research.

Despite Google's significant contributions to AI research, its products and services have faced controversies regarding privacy, algorithmic bias, and their potential effects on marginalized communities, including the Black community.

Apple

Apple, another technology giant, has been expanding its AI capabilities to enhance the user experience of its devices. One example of Apple's AI technology is Siri, the voice-activated virtual assistant integrated into its devices. However, concerns have arisen about Siri's potential to reinforce gender and racial biases in language processing, which could disproportionately impact Black users and perpetuate stereotypes.

Microsoft

Microsoft, a leading technology company, has made substantial investments in AI research and development, focusing on creating AI technologies that augment human capabilities and enhance user experience. However, Microsoft has faced criticism for its facial recognition technology due to significant racial and gender biases, raising concerns about its potential impact on the Black community.

IBM

IBM, a multinational technology and consulting corporation, has a long history of innovation in AI research, including the development of IBM Watson. IBM has been actively involved in various AI projects across industries but has faced criticism for the potential ethical implications of its AI technologies, such as the use of Watson in predictive policing, which could disproportionately affect Black communities.

Amazon

Amazon, a global e-commerce and technology company, has been actively engaged in AI research and development, spanning a wide range of applications. Amazon's AI-powered virtual assistant, Alexa, showcases their work in this field. However, Alexa has encountered criticism due to potential biases in its language processing, which might negatively impact Black users. Additionally, Amazon's facial recognition technology, Rekognition, has been criticized for its inaccuracies in identifying people of color, particularly Black individuals.

1.2 Academic and Research Institutions

Stanford University, MIT, Carnegie Mellon University (CMU), and the University of California, Berkeley have all been key players in AI research since the field's inception, making significant contributions to AI development. These institutions have increasingly focused on addressing the ethical and social implications of AI, including issues of bias, fairness, and accountability that affect the Black community.

1.3 Non-Profit and Advocacy Organizations

OpenAI, Partnership on AI (PAI), Algorithmic Justice League (AJL), and AI Now Institute are all non-profit organizations founded to ensure that AI benefits all of humanity, promote the responsible development and use of AI, and raise public awareness about the social implications of AI. They have been active in addressing the ethical and societal implications of AI, including concerns about algorithmic bias and discrimination that affect the Black community.

By understanding the organizations shaping the AI landscape, their goals, and their strategies, we gain valuable insights into the forces shaping the development and deployment of AI technologies. As AI technologies become increasingly integrated into our daily lives, it is crucial to remain informed and engaged in the AI conversation to ensure that AI technologies are developed and deployed responsibly and equitably, and

that the benefits of AI are shared by all members of society,
including Black individuals.

5

The AI Engine: Algorithms, Data, and the Magic of Machine Learning

The rapid development of AI has initiated a significant shift in how technology interacts with the world. This revolution hinges on three primary components: algorithms, data, and machine learning. This chapter delves into these crucial elements, discussing how they work together to create advanced AI technologies that are transforming the lives of Black individuals and communities.

5.1 Algorithms: The Building Blocks of AI

An algorithm is a step-by-step procedure or a set of rules for solving a problem or completing a task. In the context of AI, algorithms are the mathematical formulas and logical instructions that allow computers to process information, make decisions, and learn from experience. They serve as the backbone of AI systems, guiding how technology interacts with data and the environment.

Algorithms vary in form and complexity, each designed for a specific purpose or problem-solving. In AI, the focus is often on developing algorithms that learn from data, adapt to new situations, and enhance their performance over time.

5.2 Data: The Fuel for AI Systems

Data is the raw material that powers AI systems. It comprises input information that algorithms process and learn from to generate insights, predictions, and decisions. In AI, data can be structured (such as spreadsheets and databases) or unstructured (such as text, images, and videos).

The quality and quantity of data used in AI systems play a critical role in determining their performance and accuracy. High-quality data is essential for AI algorithms to learn patterns and make accurate predictions, particularly for machine learning algorithms that rely on vast amounts of data to train and refine their models.

For Black communities, data has a dual nature, presenting both opportunities and obstacles. AI systems have the potential to harness vast quantities of data to reveal concealed patterns and deliver valuable insights that contribute to resolving critical concerns. Nonetheless, the presence of biases and inaccuracies within data can result in AI systems that unfairly discriminate and exacerbate existing disparities and injustices.

As we've previously mentioned, it's essential to recognize these challenges and work towards creating more inclusive and accurate data sets to ensure equitable AI outcomes.

5.3 Machine Learning: The Art of Teaching Computers to Learn

Machine learning is a subfield of AI that focuses on developing algorithms enabling computers to learn from data and improve their performance over time. Instead of being explicitly programmed to perform a specific task, machine learning algorithms learn by example, using data to build models and make predictions or decisions.

Machine learning can be broadly classified into three categories: supervised learning, unsupervised learning, and reinforcement learning. Additionally, semi-supervised learning combines elements of both supervised and unsupervised learning to improve algorithm performance when labeled data is scarce.

5.4 Deep Learning: Unraveling the Complexities of Neural Networks

Deep learning, a subfield of machine learning, focuses on neural networks with many layers, known as deep neural networks. These networks can learn complex patterns and representations from large amounts of data, making them particularly well-suited for tasks involving images, text, and other high-dimensional data.

Neural networks are loosely inspired by the human brain's structure, consisting of interconnected nodes or neurons organized into layers. The deep learning revolution has been driven by several factors, including the availability of large datasets, powerful computing hardware, and advances in neural network architectures and training techniques.

5.5 AI in the Real World: Expanding Horizons

AI technologies have permeated various industries and domains, impacting every aspect of our lives. Some notable examples include transportation, entertainment, retail, manufacturing, agriculture, environment, and social impact.

Transportation

Autonomous vehicles rely on advanced AI systems to navigate, avoid obstacles, and make real-time decisions. Moreover, AI is being used to optimize traffic flow, improve public transportation systems, and even develop innovative solutions like flying taxis.

Entertainment

AI is enhancing the entertainment industry, from video games and virtual reality to content recommendation systems and even AI-generated art and music. These innovations create immersive and engaging experiences for users, pushing the boundaries of creativity and personalization.

Retail

AI is revolutionizing retail through applications such as personalized recommendations, inventory management, and pricing optimization. Additionally, AI-powered chatbots provide customer support and enhance the overall shopping experience by offering tailored suggestions and assistance.

Manufacturing

AI helps optimize production processes, detect defects in products, and automate quality control. Predictive maintenance algorithms anticipate equipment failures and schedule repairs, reducing downtime and increasing efficiency.

Agriculture

AI-driven technologies, such as drones and autonomous machinery, monitor crop health, optimize irrigation, and manage pests. AI can also help farmers make data-driven decisions to maximize crop yields and reduce environmental impact.

Environment

AI is leveraged to monitor and predict natural disasters, track wildlife populations, and optimize energy consumption in buildings and cities. These applications contribute to environmental conservation efforts and help mitigate the effects of climate change.

Social Impact

AI is being used to tackle pressing social issues, such as poverty, hunger, and climate change, by analyzing data and generating insights to inform policy and decision-making. In the context of Black communities, AI can be a powerful tool for promoting social justice, uncovering hidden biases, and driving positive change.

As AI continues to advance and its applications proliferate, the potential benefits for Black communities are vast. It is essential to recognize and address the challenges AI can pose, such as algorithmic bias and digital exclusion, to ensure these technologies are used equitably and responsibly. By fostering an inclusive AI landscape, we can unlock the transformative potential of AI and create a brighter future for all.

In this chapter, we explored the widespread applications of AI across various industries and the potential benefits they offer. As we continue to investigate the impact of AI on Black individuals and society, it's crucial to ensure that these technologies are developed and implemented responsibly, ethically, and inclusively.

6

Deep Dive into Deep Learning: Unveiling the Secrets of Neural Networks

Deep learning is a subfield of machine learning, which is itself a subfield of artificial intelligence. The key distinction between deep learning and other machine learning techniques lies in the architecture of the models used. Deep learning employs artificial neural networks, which are designed to mimic the structure and function of the human brain to process and learn from vast amounts of data.

In this chapter, we will delve deep into the inner workings of neural networks, exploring their architecture, how they learn from data, and their role in driving recent advancements in AI. We will also discuss the implications of these advancements for the Black community, highlighting both the potential benefits and the challenges that come with widespread adoption of deep learning technologies.

6.1 The Human Brain as Inspiration: Artificial Neural Networks

The human brain has long been a source of fascination and inspiration for scientists and engineers working in the field of AI. Comprised of billions of neurons, the brain is capable of processing vast amounts of information and learning from experiences in ways that are still not fully understood. To harness this incredible capacity for learning, researchers have sought to develop artificial neural networks (ANNs) that can replicate, to some extent, the structure and function of the human brain.

An artificial neural network is a computational model that consists of interconnected nodes or neurons, which are organized into layers. These neurons are responsible for processing information and passing it along to other neurons within the network. There are three main types of layers in a neural network.

Input layer

This is the first layer of the network, which receives the raw data as input. Each neuron in the input layer corresponds to a feature or attribute of the input data, such as a pixel in an image or a word in a text.

Hidden layer(s)

These are the layers between the input and output layers. They are responsible for processing and transforming the input data through a series of mathematical operations. The number of hidden layers and the number of neurons in each layer can vary, depending on the complexity of the problem and the architecture of the neural network.

Output layer

This is the final layer of the network, which produces the desired output, such as a classification or a prediction. The number of neurons in the output layer typically corresponds to the number of possible output classes or categories.

The connections between neurons in a neural network are associated with weights, which represent the strength of the connection between the neurons. These weights are initially set to random values and are adjusted during the learning process to minimize the error between the network's predictions and the actual output.

6.2 How Neural Networks Learn: The Backpropagation Algorithm

One of the key challenges in developing effective neural networks is finding a way to train them to learn from data. The most widely used algorithm for training neural networks is the backpropagation algorithm, which relies on a technique called gradient descent to minimize the error between the network's predictions and the actual output.

The backpropagation algorithm consists of two main steps:

Forward pass

During the forward pass, the input data is fed into the network, and the output is computed by propagating the data through the layers. This involves applying a series of mathematical operations, including multiplication by the weights and the application of activation functions, which determine how the neuron's output should be transformed before being passed to the next layer.

Backward pass

Once the output has been computed, the error between the network's predictions and the actual output is calculated. This error is then used to update the weights of the connections between neurons, working backward from the output layer to the input layer. This process involves computing the gradient of the error with respect to the weights, which indicates the direction in which the weights should be adjusted to minimize the error.

The backpropagation algorithm is typically performed iteratively, with the neural network processing multiple examples from the training dataset and updating its weights after each example. This iterative process is repeated until a specified stopping criterion is met, such as reaching a maximum number of iterations or achieving a desired level of accuracy on the training dataset.

6.3 Activation Functions: The Nonlinear Element

Activation functions play a crucial role in the functioning of neural networks, introducing nonlinearity into the system and enabling the network to learn complex, nonlinear relationships between inputs and outputs. Without activation functions, neural networks would be limited to learning only linear relationships, which would significantly restrict their applicability to real-world problems.

There are several commonly used activation functions in deep learning, each with its unique properties and characteristics:

- Sigmoid: The sigmoid function is a smooth, S-shaped curve that maps input values to outputs between 0 and 1. It is often used in the output layer of binary classification problems, where the goal is to predict one of two possible classes.

- Hyperbolic tangent (tanh): The tanh function is similar to the sigmoid function, but it maps input values to outputs between -1 and 1. This function is often used in hidden layers of neural networks, as it provides a wider range of output values than the sigmoid function.

- Rectified linear unit (ReLU): The ReLU function is defined as the maximum of 0 and the input value. This means that it outputs the input value if it is positive, and 0 otherwise. ReLU is computationally efficient and has become the default activation function for many deep learning models, especially in convolutional neural networks.

- Leaky ReLU: The leaky ReLU function is a variation of the ReLU function that allows for a small, non-zero output for negative input values. This can help mitigate the "dying ReLU" problem, where neurons with negative inputs become inactive and cease to contribute to the learning process.

6.4 Convolutional Neural Networks: Pioneers of the Deep Learning Revolution

Convolutional neural networks (CNNs) are a specialized type of neural network architecture designed specifically for processing grid-like data, such as images, video frames, or spectrograms. CNNs have been instrumental in driving the deep learning revolution, achieving state-of-the-art results in a wide range of computer vision tasks, such as image classification, object detection, and semantic segmentation.

The key innovation in CNNs is the use of convolutional layers, which are designed to detect local patterns or features in the input data by applying a set of filters, or kernels, across the input. These filters are capable of detecting specific patterns, such as edges, corners, or textures, and can be learned by the network during the training process. By stacking multiple convolutional layers, a CNN can learn to detect increasingly complex and abstract features in the input data.

Another important component of CNNs is the pooling layer, which is used to reduce the spatial dimensions of the input data, effectively compressing the information while preserving the most important features. Pooling layers are typically inserted between successive convolutional layers and help to reduce the computational complexity of the network.

6.5 Implications of Deep Learning and Neural Networks for the Black Community

The advancements in deep learning and neural networks have had significant implications for the Black community, both positive and negative. To ensure that the benefits of deep learning and neural networks are equitably distributed, it is crucial for the Black community to be actively involved in the development, deployment, and oversight of these technologies. This involvement includes representation in the AI research community, as well as advocating for transparency, fairness, and accountability in AI systems.

Furthermore, education and training in AI and deep learning should be made accessible to Black individuals, empowering them to participate in the development of these technologies and to harness their potential for positive change. By promoting diversity and inclusion in AI, we can work towards creating a more equitable and just society that benefits all its members.

In the upcoming chapters, we will delve deeper into the various aspects of AI and their specific implications for the Black community, exploring topics such as algorithmic discrimination, the impact of AI on the job market, and the ethical considerations surrounding the development and deployment of AI systems. Through this exploration, we aim to provide a comprehensive understanding of the challenges and opportunities that AI presents for Black individuals, as well as guidance on how to navigate this rapidly evolving landscape.

In this chapter, we took a deep dive into the world of deep learning, unveiling the secrets of neural networks that have been the driving force behind many recent advancements in AI. We explored the structure and function of artificial neural networks, inspired by the human brain, and how they enable machines to process and learn from vast amounts of data.

We discussed the key components of neural networks, including neurons, layers, and activation functions, as well as the process of forward and backward propagation that allows for learning and optimization. We also examined the various types of neural networks, such as feedforward, recurrent, and convolutional neural networks, each designed for specific tasks and applications.

As we concluded this chapter, we have gained a deeper understanding of the power and potential of deep learning in revolutionizing various fields and industries. With this knowledge, we are better prepared to assess the impact of AI on the lives of Black individuals and explore the ethical implications and challenges that come with the widespread adoption of this transformative technology.

7

Learning by Trial and Triumph: The World of Reinforcement Learning

Reinforcement learning is a paradigm in the field of AI that has gained increasing attention and recognition in recent years. It is a subfield of machine learning, where an agent learns to make decisions by interacting with an environment, receiving feedback in the form of rewards or penalties, and using this feedback to improve its decision-making over time.

This chapter will delve into the fascinating world of reinforcement learning, exploring its foundations, various algorithms and techniques, and real-world applications. By the end of this chapter, the reader will have a comprehensive understanding of reinforcement learning and its significance in the landscape of AI, especially for Black individuals and communities.

7.1 Foundations of Reinforcement Learning

The roots of reinforcement learning can be traced back to early research in psychology, specifically the work of B.F. Skinner on operant conditioning. In this paradigm, an organism learns to associate actions with their consequences, leading to the reinforcement of desirable behaviors and the suppression of undesirable ones.

Reinforcement learning takes inspiration from this concept and formalizes it within a mathematical framework. The key components of a reinforcement learning problem are:

- Agent: The entity that makes decisions and takes actions in the environment.
- Environment: The context within which the agent operates and interacts.
- State: A representation of the current situation or context of the agent in the environment.
- Action: A decision made by the agent that affects its state within the environment.
- Reward: A scalar value received by the agent as feedback for its actions, indicating the desirability of the outcome.

The agent's goal in a reinforcement learning problem is to maximize the cumulative rewards it receives over time. This is achieved by learning a policy, which is a mapping from states to actions, that guides the agent's decision-making process.

7.2 Key Concepts in Reinforcement Learning

Several key concepts and techniques form the backbone of reinforcement learning.

Exploration vs. Exploitation

A crucial challenge faced by reinforcement learning agents is balancing the need to explore new actions and states to learn about their potential rewards (exploration) and leveraging the knowledge acquired so far to make the best decisions (exploitation). Striking the right balance between these two objectives is essential for achieving optimal performance.

Value Functions

These functions estimate the expected long-term return (cumulative rewards) for an agent in a given state or state-action pair. Value functions are central to many reinforcement learning algorithms, as they help the agent to evaluate the desirability of different actions and guide its decision-making.

Temporal Difference Learning

This is a class of algorithms that learn by bootstrapping, or updating value function estimates based on the differences between successive predictions. Temporal difference learning methods, such as Q-learning and SARSA, are widely used in reinforcement learning due to their ability to learn online, i.e., without requiring a complete model of the environment.

Model-Free vs. Model-Based Approaches

Reinforcement learning algorithms can be broadly classified into two categories based on how they learn and make decisions. Model-free approaches, such as Q-learning and policy gradients, learn directly from interaction with the environment, without explicitly modeling the dynamics of the environment. In contrast, model-based approaches attempt to learn a model of the environment and use this model to plan and make decisions.

Function Approximation

In many real-world problems, the state and action spaces are large or continuous, making it infeasible to represent value functions or policies explicitly. Function approximation techniques, such as neural networks, are used to represent and learn these functions in a compact and generalizable form.

7.3 Reinforcement Learning Algorithms

Reinforcement learning boasts a diverse array of algorithms and techniques that cater to different problem settings and requirements.

Q-learning

This is a model-free, value-based algorithm that learns an action-value function, representing the expected return for taking a specific action in a given state. Q-learning iteratively updates its estimates based on the observed rewards and transitions in the environment and converges to the optimal action-value function under certain conditions.

SARSA (State-Action-Reward-State-Action)

Another model-free, value-based algorithm, SARSA is an on-policy method that learns the action-value function for the current policy, i.e., the policy followed by the agent while learning. SARSA updates its estimates based on the actual actions taken by the agent, making it more conservative than Q-learning, which updates based on the best possible action in the next state.

Deep Q-Networks (DQN)

This algorithm combines Q-learning with deep neural networks to tackle high-dimensional state spaces and learn value functions in a more scalable and generalizable manner. DQN introduced several innovations, such as experience replay and target networks, which have become standard techniques in deep reinforcement learning.

Policy Gradient Methods

These are a class of model-free, policy-based algorithms that learn a parametric representation of the policy directly. Policy gradient methods optimize the policy parameters by following the gradient of the expected return with respect to the parameters. Notable policy gradient algorithms include REINFORCE, TRPO (Trust Region Policy Optimization), and PPO (Proximal Policy Optimization).

Actor-Critic Methods

These algorithms combine the best of both worlds – value-based and policy-based approaches – by learning both a value function (the critic) and a policy (the actor). The critic is used to evaluate and guide the learning of the actor, leading to more stable and efficient learning. Examples of actor-critic methods include A2C (Advantage Actor-Critic) and DDPG (Deep Deterministic Policy Gradient).

7.4 Applications of Reinforcement Learning

Reinforcement learning has been successfully applied to a wide range of real-world problems, showcasing its versatility and potential.

Robotics

Reinforcement learning has been employed to teach robots various tasks, such as grasping objects, walking, and flying, by learning from trial and error. The ability to learn autonomously makes reinforcement learning a promising tool for enabling robots to adapt to new situations and environments.

Game Playing

One of the most publicized successes of reinforcement learning has been in the domain of game playing. AlphaGo, developed by DeepMind, utilized a combination of deep neural networks and reinforcement learning to defeat the world champion in the game of Go, a feat previously thought to be decades away. Reinforcement learning has also shown remarkable performance in classic board games like chess and shogi, as well as video games like Atari and StarCraft.

Finance

Reinforcement learning has been applied to various problems in finance, such as portfolio management, trading, and risk management. By learning to make decisions in uncertain and dynamic environments, reinforcement learning algorithms can help optimize financial strategies and navigate complex market dynamics.

Healthcare

Reinforcement learning has the potential to revolutionize healthcare by optimizing treatment plans, personalizing medical interventions, and assisting in drug discovery. For example, reinforcement learning can be used to develop optimal dosing strategies for patients, taking into account their individual characteristics and response to treatment.

Smart Grids

Reinforcement learning can be employed to optimize energy consumption and distribution in smart grids, leading to more efficient and sustainable energy management. By learning to balance supply and demand, reinforcement learning algorithms can help minimize energy waste and reduce costs for both consumers and providers.

These applications illustrate the tremendous potential of reinforcement learning in addressing a wide range of complex and dynamic problems. The ability of reinforcement learning agents to learn and adapt through trial and error makes them particularly well-suited for tackling challenges in domains where explicit programming of rules is infeasible or impractical. As the field of reinforcement learning continues to advance, we can expect to see even more innovative and impactful applications across various domains.

7.5 The Future of Reinforcement Learning for Black Individuals and Communities

As AI technologies continue to develop and permeate different aspects of our lives, it is essential to consider their impact on marginalized communities, such as Black individuals and communities. Reinforcement learning, with its ability to learn and adapt in complex environments, offers significant potential for addressing challenges and improving the quality of life in these communities.

Some possible avenues for leveraging reinforcement learning
to benefit Black individuals and communities include:

- Education: Reinforcement learning can be used to develop personalized learning systems that adapt to individual students' needs and learning styles. This could help to close the achievement gap and provide better educational opportunities for Black students.
- Economic empowerment: Reinforcement learning can be applied to areas such as job training, skill development, and small business support, helping to create more equitable economic opportunities for Black individuals and communities.
- Community health: Reinforcement learning can be harnessed to optimize public health interventions and resource allocation in underserved communities, leading to improved health outcomes and a reduction in health disparities.
- Smart cities: Reinforcement learning can be utilized to optimize urban planning and resource management in Black communities, leading to more sustainable, efficient, and livable cities.

As we wrap up this chapter on reinforcement learning, we
have explored the foundations, algorithms, and applications
of this rapidly evolving field within AI. With its potential
to address complex and dynamic problems across various
domains, understanding reinforcement learning is essential in

appreciating its significance and the potential impact it holds for the world.

With a focus on Black individuals and communities, it is crucial to ensure that the development and deployment of reinforcement learning technologies are inclusive and sensitive to their needs and aspirations. This requires the combined efforts of researchers, policymakers, and industry stakeholders to promote diversity and representation in AI, engage with affected communities, and work towards the equitable distribution of these technologies' benefits.

Armed with a comprehensive understanding of reinforcement learning and its role in shaping the future of AI, we are now better equipped to evaluate the ethical and societal implications associated with the increasing prevalence of intelligent machines in our lives and their impact on Black communities.

8

The AI Spectrum: From Rule-Based Systems to Advanced Neural Networks

8.1 Unveiling the AI Spectrum

Grasping the influence of artificial intelligence (AI) on society, particularly Black communities, necessitates a deep understanding of the diverse AI systems that exist, their capabilities, and limitations. AI technologies have evolved over time, from basic rule-based systems to advanced neural networks capable of learning from new information. This chapter offers a thorough examination of various AI systems, their underlying concepts, and potential consequences for Black individuals and communities.

8.2 The Foundations: Rule-Based Systems and AI's Infancy

Rule-based systems, otherwise known as symbolic AI or expert systems, were among the pioneering AI methods. These systems rely on explicitly programmed rules that determine AI behavior, often represented as IF-THEN statements that define responses to specific conditions.

For instance, a rule-based system for diagnosing illnesses could include rules like:

- IF the patient has a fever AND a cough, THEN they may have the flu.
- IF the patient has chest pain AND shortness of breath, THEN they may have a heart attack.

Although once considered promising for replicating human expertise in specific domains, rule-based systems have limitations that prompted the development of alternative AI approaches:

- Scalability: Increasing complexity in problem domains leads to an unmanageable number of rules required to cover all situations, complicating rule base maintenance and consistency.
- Brittleness: Rule-based systems often fail to handle unanticipated situations, making them prone to failure when confronted with novel or unexpected inputs.
- Knowledge acquisition: Developing a rule set for a rule-based system generally demands significant domain ex-

pertise, which can be time-consuming, costly, and error-prone.

Nonetheless, rule-based systems remain useful for well-defined problem domains with easily captured knowledge. They have been employed in legal analysis, educational software, and financial planning, helping address disparities and promote equity in Black communities.

8.3 The Next Frontier: Machine Learning and Data-Driven AI

As rule-based systems' limitations became clear, researchers started exploring alternative AI approaches, such as machine learning. Machine learning algorithms learn and improve performance through exposure to data, adapting to new information and making predictions or decisions based on data patterns rather than explicit rules.

Machine learning has significantly impacted various applications, from self-driving cars to personalized medicine. However, it is essential to recognize that machine learning algorithms can exhibit biases, particularly when trained on data reflecting societal disparities.

8.4 The Cutting Edge: Deep Learning and Neural Networks

Deep learning, a machine learning subset, focuses on artificial neural networks—computational models inspired by human brain structure and function. Neural networks consist of interconnected layers of nodes or neurons that process and transmit information through weighted connections. By adjusting connection weights during training, neural networks can represent complex patterns and relationships in input data.

Deep learning has garnered attention due to its exceptional performance on various tasks, particularly those involving large-scale data and high-dimensional inputs, such as image and speech recognition. The success of deep learning can be attributed to several factors, including advances in computational power, the availability of large datasets for training, and the development of novel neural network architectures and training techniques.

8.5 A Holistic Approach: Hybrid AI Systems

As AI research has advanced, it has become evident that no single AI approach can address the full range of real-world problems and challenges. Consequently, many AI systems today combine elements of rule-based systems, machine learning, and deep learning to achieve optimal performance.

Hybrid AI systems can take advantage of each approach's strengths while mitigating their respective weaknesses. For instance, a hybrid system might use rule-based reasoning to manage well-defined aspects of a problem, while relying on machine learning or deep learning techniques to adapt and improve its performance in more complex or uncertain situations.

As this chapter comes to a close, we have explored the various types of AI systems, delving into their unique attributes and potential applications. Our exploration of rule-based systems, machine learning, deep learning, and hybrid AI systems has provided us with valuable insights that will enable us to better assess the consequences of AI on Black communities, as well as other underrepresented populations. This knowledge equips us to participate in essential conversations about AI's influence in our world and empowers us to make well-informed choices as we strive to create an inclusive and equitable future for all.

9

The AI Classroom: Training Machines to Learn from Data

9.1 Introduction

One crucial aspect of AI is its ability to learn from data. The process of training machine learning algorithms enables AI systems to develop their capabilities and improve their performance over time. In this chapter, we will explore the training process of machine learning algorithms, including the methods used, the challenges faced, and the implications for the Black community.

9.2 The Basics of Machine Learning

To understand the training process, let's briefly revisit the basic concepts of machine learning. Machine learning is a subfield of

AI that focuses on developing algorithms that allow computers to learn from and make predictions or decisions based on data. Machine learning can be categorized into three main types: supervised learning, unsupervised learning, and reinforcement learning.

9.3 The Training Process

The training process of machine learning algorithms typically involves several steps, including data preparation, model selection, model training, and model evaluation.

Data Preparation

Data preparation is a crucial step in the machine learning process, as the quality of the data used for training directly impacts the performance of the resulting model. This stage involves several tasks, such as data collection, data cleaning, and data preprocessing.

Data Collection

The first step in data preparation is collecting the data that will be used to train the algorithm. In many cases, this involves gathering large quantities of raw data from various sources, such as sensors, databases, or the internet. The type and amount of data collected depend on the specific problem being addressed and the machine learning technique being used.

Data Cleaning

Once the data has been collected, it must be cleaned to ensure its quality and consistency. Data cleaning involves identifying and correcting errors, inconsistencies, and inaccuracies in the data. This may include removing duplicate records, filling in missing values, correcting data entry errors, and addressing any other issues that could negatively impact the performance of the machine learning model.

Data Preprocessing

After cleaning the data, it must be preprocessed to prepare it for use in the machine learning algorithm. This may involve tasks such as transforming the data into a suitable format, normalizing or scaling the data, and encoding categorical variables. Additionally, data preprocessing may include feature engineering, which involves creating new, derived features from the raw data to improve the algorithm's ability to learn patterns and make predictions.

Model Selection

Once the data has been prepared, the next step is selecting an appropriate machine learning model for the problem at hand. Model selection involves choosing the type of algorithm (e.g., linear regression, decision tree, neural network) and determining the model's hyperparameters, which are the settings that govern the model's behavior. The choice of model and hyperparameters depends on various factors, including the type of problem being addressed, the nature of the data, and the desired performance characteristics.

Model Training

With the data prepared and the model selected, the next step is to train the machine learning model. During the training process, the algorithm iteratively adjusts its internal parameters to minimize the discrepancy between its predictions and the actual output values in the training data. This process is often referred to as "learning" or "fitting" the model to the data.

The training process can be computationally intensive and may take a significant amount of time, especially for large datasets and complex models. Various optimization techniques are employed to speed up the training process, such as gradient descent, which is a popular method for finding the optimal set of model parameters that minimize the error between the model's predictions and the actual data.

Model Evaluation

After the model has been trained, it is essential to evaluate its performance on new, unseen data to assess its ability to generalize beyond the training set. This typically involves splitting the data into separate training and testing sets, where the model is trained on one subset of the data and evaluated on the other. Common evaluation metrics include accuracy, precision, recall, and F1 score for classification tasks and mean squared error, mean absolute error, and R-squared for regression tasks.

9.4 Challenges in the Training Process

The training process of machine learning algorithms can be fraught with challenges, including overfitting, underfitting, and bias in the data.

Overfitting and Underfitting

Overfitting occurs when a model becomes too specialized to the training data, capturing not only the underlying patterns but also the noise present in the data. This results in poor performance when applied to new, unseen data. On the other hand, underfitting occurs when the model is not complex enough to capture the underlying patterns in the data, resulting in poor performance on both the training and testing sets.

To combat these issues, various techniques can be employed, such as regularization, which adds a penalty term to the model's complexity to encourage simpler models, and cross-validation, which involves dividing the data into multiple folds and training and evaluating the model on each fold to assess its ability to generalize.

Bias in the Data

Another challenge in the training process is the presence of bias in the data. Bias can be introduced during the data collection process or result from an unbalanced representation of different groups within the dataset. Algorithmic and AI discrimination can have significant consequences for the Black community, as biased data can lead to biased predictions and perpetuate existing inequalities.

To address this issue, it is essential to carefully consider the data collection process, ensure fair representation of different groups, and employ techniques such as re-sampling or weighting to balance the data.

9.5 Implications for the Black Community

As AI continues to permeate various aspects of society, it is crucial to understand the training process and its potential impact on the Black community. By being aware of the challenges and potential biases in the training process, individuals and organizations can work to ensure that AI systems are developed and deployed in a manner that promotes fairness, equity, and inclusion.

In this chapter, we delved into the AI classroom, exploring the processes and techniques that enable machines to learn from data. We examined the key concepts of data preprocessing, feature selection, and feature engineering, which are vital to preparing data for training. Additionally, we covered model evaluation and validation, which ensure that the machine learning models we create are reliable and accurate. We also discussed the importance of tuning hyperparameters and the role of cross-validation in obtaining the best model performance. By understanding these essential aspects of the machine learning process, we can appreciate how AI systems are trained and refined, and ultimately, how they can learn and adapt from the data we provide.

In the next chapter, we will explore real-world examples of AI in action and the potential benefits and challenges that these applications present for the Black community.

10

AI in Action: Real-World Examples of Artificial Intelligence Transforming Lives

10.1 Introduction

AI has rapidly become an integral part of our daily lives, with applications spanning across numerous sectors, including healthcare, finance, transportation, and education. In this chapter, we will explore real-world examples of AI transforming lives, showcasing its positive impact on society, as well as potential risks and challenges. We will also discuss the importance of considering the implications of AI on the Black community, ensuring that AI technologies promote equity, inclusivity, and fairness.

10.2 Healthcare

AI has made significant advancements in the healthcare sector, with applications ranging from diagnostics and treatment to drug discovery and personalized medicine.

One notable example is Google's DeepMind, which developed an AI system called AlphaFold. This groundbreaking technology predicts protein structures with remarkable accuracy, a problem that has puzzled scientists for decades. Accurate protein structure prediction is crucial for understanding diseases and developing new drugs. AlphaFold's success has the potential to accelerate drug discovery and bring life-saving treatments to market faster. [1]

Another example is the use of AI in medical imaging. AI algorithms have shown great promise in accurately detecting and diagnosing various medical conditions, such as cancer, cardiovascular diseases, and neurological disorders. For instance, researchers at Stanford University developed an AI algorithm that can detect skin cancer with a level of accuracy comparable to dermatologists. [2] Similarly, Zebra Medical Vision, an Israeli startup, uses AI to analyze medical imaging data and detect early signs of diseases such as breast cancer, lung cancer, and liver disease. [3]

AI-driven healthcare advancements hold promise in enhancing access to quality healthcare for marginalized communities, including the Black community. It remains crucial to train AI algorithms on diverse data, thereby mitigating the risk of perpetuating biases and disparities in healthcare outcomes.

10.3 Finance

The financial sector has also witnessed a growing adoption of AI technologies, with applications in areas such as credit scoring, fraud detection, and algorithmic trading.

AI-powered credit scoring models, such as those developed by companies like Zest AI and Upstart, aim to make credit more accessible to underserved populations by leveraging alternative data sources and sophisticated machine learning algorithms. These models consider various factors beyond traditional credit scores, such as employment history, education, and income, providing a more comprehensive assessment of a borrower's creditworthiness. This can potentially increase access to credit for marginalized communities, including the Black community, who have historically faced systemic barriers in obtaining loans and financial services. [4]

There exists a risk that AI algorithms, if not carefully designed and monitored, may inadvertently perpetuate existing biases and discrimination. A 2018 study revealed that an AI-based lending model employed by a prominent online lender demonstrated racial disparities. Black and Hispanic applicants experienced a lower probability of receiving loans compared to their White counterparts, even after accounting for creditworthiness. [5]

10.4 Transportation

AI has revolutionized transportation, with the development of self-driving cars, optimized traffic management systems, and intelligent transportation infrastructure.

Companies like Tesla, Waymo, and Cruise are at the forefront of developing autonomous vehicles that rely on AI algorithms to perceive their environment, make decisions, and navigate complex traffic situations. The widespread adoption of self-driving cars has the potential to reduce traffic accidents, improve road safety, and enhance mobility for those who cannot drive, such as the elderly and disabled. [6]

Concerns have arisen regarding potential biases in AI systems used in autonomous vehicles. A study conducted by researchers from the Georgia Institute of Technology discovered that object detection algorithms in self-driving cars were less accurate in detecting pedestrians with darker skin tones. This emphasizes the necessity for rigorous testing and validation of AI algorithms in safety-critical applications to guarantee fairness and prevent the perpetuation of existing disparities. [7]

10.5 Education

AI is transforming the education sector by enabling personalized learning, improving student assessment and feedback, and enhancing teaching resources.

One example is Carnegie Learning's MATHia, an AI-driven math tutoring platform that provides personalized instruction and real-time feedback to students. MATHia adapts to each student's learning pace, identifying areas of weakness, and offering targeted support. [8] Similarly, Thinkster Math, another AI-driven platform, uses machine learning algorithms to analyze student performance and provide tailored feedback and recommendations.[9]

AI applications in education have the potential to bridge the gap in educational outcomes for underprivileged communities, including the Black community. It is vital to ensure that AI systems are designed with cultural sensitivity and do not inadvertently perpetuate biases or stereotypes.

In this chapter, we explored AI in action by examining real-world examples of AI transforming lives across various sectors. From healthcare, education, and finance, to transportation, criminal justice, and the environment, we witnessed the incredible potential of AI to reshape industries and improve the quality of life for people around the world. These case studies highlighted the breadth and depth of AI's impact on society, demonstrating its ability to revolutionize traditional processes, solve complex problems, and offer innovative solutions. As we continue to embrace AI's possibilities, it is essential to remain aware of its potential risks and challenges, ensuring that its development and deployment remain ethical, transparent, and equitable for all.

11

Unveiling Bias: Algorithmic and AI Discrimination in the Digital Age

11.1 Introduction

AI and machine learning technologies hold the potential to bring about transformative changes in various aspects of our lives. Nonetheless, these technologies can still reflect biases present in the data used for their training. The consequences of algorithmic discrimination can be significant, impacting marginalized communities, including Black individuals, in a considerable manner. In this chapter, we will delve into several case studies that showcase the presence of bias in AI systems, and discuss potential solutions to tackle and alleviate these concerns.

11.2 Gender Shades: Intersectional Accuracy Disparities in Commercial Gender Classification

The Gender Shades project, led by Joy Buolamwini and Timnit Gebru, assessed the accuracy of commercial facial recognition systems, including those from IBM, Microsoft, and Face++. The researchers found significant disparities in accuracy between lighter-skinned males and darker-skinned females, with the highest error rates for darker-skinned females. [10]

These disparities in AI performance could lead to harmful consequences for the affected groups, including misidentification, exclusion from services, and violations of privacy rights.

11.3 Amazon's Face Recognition Falsely Matched Members of Congress with Mugshots

In 2018, the American Civil Liberties Union (ACLU) conducted a study using Amazon's facial recognition technology, Rekognition, and discovered that it falsely matched 28 members of Congress with criminal mugshots. The false matches disproportionately affected people of color, demonstrating a concerning bias in the system. [11]

This case highlights the potential for AI-based facial recognition to perpetuate racial profiling and discrimination in law enforcement and other sectors.

11.4 Predictive Policing: To Predict and Serve?

The use of AI in predictive policing has raised concerns about racial biases in these systems. Lum and Isaac analyzed the algorithm used in a predictive policing system called PredPol. They discovered that the system had a tendency to over-predict crime in predominantly Black neighborhoods while under-predicting crime in predominantly white neighborhoods. [12]

11.5 Machine Bias in Criminal Sentencing

In 2016, ProPublica published an investigative report on the risk assessment algorithm used in the criminal justice system in the United States. The algorithm, called COMPAS, was found to disproportionately label Black defendants as higher risk for recidivism, while white defendants were more likely to be labeled as lower risk. [13]

This bias in the algorithm can lead to harsher sentencing and longer incarceration times for Black individuals.

11.6 Amazon's AI Recruiting Tool Showing Bias Against Women

Reuters reported in 2018 that Amazon had scrapped an AI recruiting tool that showed bias against women. The tool was designed to review job applicants' resumes and provide recommendations to recruiters. The algorithm displayed a preference for male applicants since it was trained on predominantly male resumes submitted to the company during a ten-year period. [14]

This instance demonstrates the potential for AI systems to reinforce existing biases in the workforce, obstructing diversity and equal opportunity.

11.7 Discrimination Through Optimization: Facebook's Ad Delivery

In a study conducted by Ali et al., researchers found that Facebook's ad delivery system could lead to skewed outcomes and discrimination. The study revealed that ads for housing and employment opportunities were disproportionately shown to specific demographic groups, potentially violating fair housing and employment laws. [15]

This example highlights the need for transparency and accountability in AI systems to ensure that they do not perpetuate discrimination.

11.8 Discrimination in Online Ad Delivery

Sweeney conducted a study on Google's online ad delivery system, examining the prevalence of racial bias. The research found that searches for names associated with Black individuals were more likely to display ads for arrest records than searches for names associated with white individuals. [16]

This racial bias in online ad delivery could contribute to the perpetuation of negative stereotypes and have lasting consequences for affected individuals.

11.9 Racial Bias in Healthcare Algorithms

In a 2019 study, Obermeyer et al. examined racial bias in an algorithm used to manage the health of populations. The algorithm was designed to identify patients with complex health needs and allocate additional resources to them. The study discovered that the algorithm demonstrated a lower likelihood of identifying Black patients for additional care, even though their health needs were on par with white patients. [17]

Such racial bias in the healthcare algorithm has the potential to worsen existing health disparities between Black and white populations.

11.10 Addressing AI Discrimination: Challenges and Opportunities

As AI technologies continue to advance and permeate various aspects of society, it is crucial to address and mitigate the biases present in these systems. Some potential strategies to tackle AI discrimination include:

- Ensuring diverse and representative data sets: AI algorithms are only as good as the data they are trained on. By ensuring that training data is diverse and representative of the target population, we can reduce the likelihood of biased outcomes.
- Implementing fairness metrics: Developing and implementing fairness metrics during the development and evaluation of AI systems can help identify and mitigate biases.
- Encouraging transparency: Increasing transparency in the development and deployment of AI systems can facilitate public scrutiny and accountability.
- Collaborative research and interdisciplinary approaches: Researchers from various disciplines, including social sciences, ethics, and law, should collaborate in the development of AI systems to ensure a holistic understanding of the potential consequences and implications of these technologies.
- Engaging with affected communities: Involving members of marginalized communities in the development, evaluation, and governance of AI systems can help ensure that their perspectives and concerns are taken into account.

In this chapter, we delved into the critical issue of algorithmic and AI discrimination in the digital age. By analyzing various case studies, we revealed the ways in which AI systems can inadvertently perpetuate or escalate existing biases and inequalities, particularly for Black individuals and other marginalized communities.

As we unpacked the consequences of AI discrimination, we gained a deeper understanding of the importance of addressing these issues to ensure that the benefits of AI are fairly distributed, and its harms are minimized. Moving forward, it is crucial to prioritize fairness, accountability, and transparency in AI development and deployment, while also fostering a culture of inclusivity and collaboration to create a more equitable and just AI landscape for all.

12

From Digital Redlining to Digital Divides: Historical Tech Exclusion in Black Communities

12.1 Introduction

Digital redlining and the digital divide are concepts that define the unequal distribution of resources and opportunities in the digital age. These issues have roots in historical systems of discrimination and exclusion that disproportionately affect Black communities in the United States. In this chapter, we will explore the history of digital redlining and the digital divide, examine their lasting effects on Black communities, and discuss strategies for addressing these disparities.

12.2 Digital Redlining: Understanding the Concept

Digital redlining describes the systematic exclusion of certain communities from accessing digital resources, technology, or services. In the digital age, it occurs when marginalized communities, often those with a higher proportion of Black residents, face unequal access to digital resources such as high-speed internet, advanced technologies, and digital services. Digital redlining can manifest in various ways, including inadequate infrastructure, higher costs, disinvestment in technology, and discriminatory algorithms. The consequences are far-reaching, magnifying existing social and economic disparities and limiting access to education, healthcare, employment opportunities, and social services for affected communities. Addressing digital redlining requires concerted efforts from policymakers, tech companies, and community organizations.

12.3 The Origins of Digital Redlining

The term "digital redlining" is derived from the historical practice of redlining, which originated in the United States in the 1930s. Redlining was a discriminatory practice employed by banks, insurance companies, and other institutions to deny services or charge higher rates to residents of certain neighborhoods based on their racial or ethnic composition. Although the Fair Housing Act of 1968 outlawed redlining, the impact of this discriminatory practice is still felt today in Black communities across the United States, hindering their ability to accumulate wealth and access essential resources.

12.4 The Emergence of the Digital Divide

The digital divide refers to the gap between individuals, households, and communities in terms of their access to information and communication technologies (ICTs). The divide can be attributed to several factors, including socio-economic status, geographic location, and education level. Race and ethnicity play a significant role in predicting digital access and usage. As the internet became more widespread and essential, the divide expanded to include not only access but also the quality of connections, digital literacy, and the ability to leverage digital resources for social and economic advancement.

12.5 The Impact of the Digital Divide on Black Communities

The digital divide has had significant consequences for Black communities in the United States, deepening existing inequalities and hindering their ability to participate fully in the digital economy. Key areas of impact include education, employment, healthcare, civic engagement, and economic development.

12.6 Historical Tech Exclusion in Black Communities

In addition to the digital divide, historical tech exclusion has further heightened disparities faced by Black communities in the digital age. Examples of historical tech exclusion include disinvestment in infrastructure, unequal access to education and training opportunities, and discrimination in the tech industry.

12.7 Analyzing Historical Examples of Digital Redlining and Digital Divide

Several instances in history highlight the pervasive nature of digital redlining and the digital divide, emphasizing the need for concerted efforts to address these issues. These examples demonstrate the historical and ongoing impact on marginalized communities, particularly people of color.

The Telecom Act of 1996

This legislation aimed to increase competition in the telecommunications market and encourage the expansion of broadband services. However, the Act did not explicitly address the issue of digital redlining. As a result, many marginalized communities, particularly those with a high proportion of Black residents, were left behind as broadband providers focused on more profitable areas. [18]

The One Laptop per Child (OLPC) Initiative

Launched in 2005, this program aimed to provide low-cost laptops to children in developing countries to bridge the digital divide. However, the initiative faced criticism for not sufficiently addressing the broader issues surrounding digital access, such as the need for infrastructure, teacher training, and culturally relevant content. Despite its intentions, the OLPC initiative fell short in significantly reducing the digital divide. [19]

The National Broadband Plan

In 2010, the Federal Communications Commission (FCC) released the National Broadband Plan, a comprehensive strategy to expand broadband access across the United States. The plan acknowledged the digital divide's impact on marginalized communities and included several recommendations to address the issue. However, implementation challenges and insufficient funding have hampered the plan's effectiveness in fully bridging the digital divide. [20]

The ConnectED Initiative

Launched by the Obama administration in 2013, ConnectED aimed to provide high-speed internet access to 99% of K-12 students in the United States within five years. While the initiative made significant progress in expanding access to schools, it did not specifically address the digital divide that many students faced at home, particularly those from marginalized communities. [21]

The Digital Inclusion Trailblazers

This initiative, established by the National Digital Inclusion Alliance, recognizes local governments that have made significant strides in promoting digital inclusion and addressing the digital divide. While these trailblazers have successfully implemented various programs and strategies to increase digital access, the digital divide remains a persistent challenge, particularly for Black communities. [22]

These historical examples demonstrate the ongoing struggle to address digital redlining and the digital divide. While some progress has been made, a more comprehensive and targeted approach is necessary to ensure that marginalized communities, particularly people of color, have equal access to digital resources and opportunities.

12.8 Community and Government Efforts in Addressing the Digital Divide and Digital Redlining

Several community and government efforts have been implemented to address the digital divide and digital redlining, with varying degrees of success.

Community-based initiatives

Grassroots organizations and nonprofits have played a crucial role in bridging the digital divide within their communities. They have provided resources, digital skills training, and support for individuals and families to access the internet and technology. Examples include EveryoneOn, which connects low-income families to affordable internet service and devices [23], and The Digital Equity Lab, which works to advance digital equity through research, policy, and community engagement [24].

Federal government programs

The federal government has implemented several programs to address the digital divide, such as the Lifeline program, which provides discounted phone and internet services for low-income households [25], and the E-Rate program, which offers discounted internet access to schools and libraries

[26]. The American Rescue Plan Act of 2021 also allocated significant funding for broadband infrastructure and digital equity initiatives [27].

State and local government initiatives

State and local governments have also taken action to address digital redlining and the digital divide. Many cities have implemented programs to provide free or low-cost internet access to residents, such as municipal broadband networks or public Wi-Fi initiatives. Some states, like California, have established offices of broadband and digital equity to develop and implement strategies for expanding access to high-speed internet and digital resources [28].

Public-private partnerships

Collaborations between the public and private sectors can help scale up efforts to bridge the digital divide. For example, companies like Google and Microsoft have partnered with local governments and community organizations to expand broadband access and digital skills training in underserved areas [29].

In this chapter, we explored the historical context of digital redlining and the digital divide, shedding light on the roots of technological exclusion that disproportionately affect Black communities.

13

AI's Double-Edged Sword: Weighing the Pros and Cons for Black Communities

13.1 Introduction

As AI continues to permeate our daily lives, it is essential to understand the various ways it can impact different communities. For Black individuals, AI presents both tremendous opportunities and significant challenges. In this chapter, we will delve deeper into the pros and cons of AI for Black communities, examining the potential benefits and drawbacks in various aspects of life.

13.2 The Pros of AI for Black Communities

Enhancing education and learning opportunities

As previously mentioned, AI-driven educational tools hold the potential to transform learning experiences by offering personalized approaches tailored to individual needs. For Black students, who have faced historical educational disparities, these innovative tools can supply valuable support and resources, contributing to the closure of the achievement gap and the enhancement of educational outcomes.

Empowering economic growth and job creation

AI technologies can drive economic growth and create new job opportunities in various sectors. As more industries adopt AI, there is a growing demand for skilled professionals in areas such as data science, machine learning, and AI ethics. By investing in training and educational programs, Black individuals can access these high-paying jobs and contribute to the growth of the AI industry.

Improving healthcare and reducing disparities

As discussed earlier, AI can help improve healthcare outcomes by providing more accurate diagnoses, better treatment recommendations, and more efficient resource allocation. For Black communities, which often experience health disparities, AI can help address these inequalities by identifying patterns and trends in health data, enabling targeted interventions and improved healthcare access.

Advancing social justice and reducing bias

We have previously explored how AI can be used to identify and address instances of bias and discrimination in various sectors, including criminal justice, housing, and employment. By developing AI systems that prioritize fairness and transparency, we can work towards dismantling systemic racism and promoting equality for Black individuals.

13.3 The Cons of AI for Black Communities

Bias and discrimination in AI systems

As mentioned in previous chapters, AI algorithms are not free from bias, and they can continue and augment existing inequalities when not designed and deployed ethically.

Job displacement and economic inequality

While AI can create new job opportunities, it can also lead to job displacement as automation replaces human labor. The impact of job displacement may disproportionately affect Black workers, who are often overrepresented in industries with high levels of automation. Addressing this potential economic inequality will require retraining and reskilling initiatives to help Black workers transition to new roles and industries.

The digital divide and access to technology

As previously discussed, the digital divide, which refers to the gap in access to technology and internet connectivity, can hinder the benefits of AI for Black communities. Without equitable access to AI technologies, Black individuals may miss out on the opportunities AI offers in areas such as education, healthcare, and employment. Addressing this divide will require investment in infrastructure and digital literacy programs to ensure that all individuals can access and benefit from AI advancements.

Surveillance and privacy concerns

As mentioned earlier, AI-driven surveillance tools, including facial recognition and predictive policing, may disproportionately affect Black communities by reinforcing biases within law enforcement and encroaching on privacy rights. To tackle these issues, it is essential to establish ethical frameworks and regulatory measures governing AI usage in surveillance and law enforcement contexts, alongside advocating for robust privacy safeguards.

13.4 Balancing the Pros and Cons: A Path Forward

Recognizing the potential benefits and challenges of AI for Black communities is critical to ensuring that its advancements are harnessed equitably. Stakeholders, including policymakers, AI developers, educators, and community leaders, must collaborate to:

- Develop and implement AI systems that prioritize fairness, transparency, and accountability, mitigating the risks of bias and discrimination, as emphasized in earlier chapters.
- Invest in education and workforce development programs to prepare Black individuals for the AI-driven job market and ensure their representation in the AI industry.
- Address the digital divide by investing in infrastructure, technology access, and digital literacy initiatives, ensuring that Black communities can fully benefit from AI advance-

ments, as previously mentioned.

- Advocate for privacy protections and ethical guidelines in AI applications, particularly in areas such as surveillance and law enforcement, to minimize potential harm to Black individuals and communities, as discussed in earlier chapters.

By working together to address the challenges and maximize the benefits of AI, we can create a more equitable and inclusive future for Black communities in the age of intelligent machines.

In this chapter, we delved into the complexities of AI's impact on Black communities, examining both the potential benefits and the challenges it presents. We explored how AI can contribute to advancements in healthcare, education, employment, and social justice while acknowledging the risks of perpetuating biases, exacerbating economic inequality, widening the digital divide, and infringing on privacy rights, as mentioned in previous chapters.

We also highlighted the importance of a collaborative approach among stakeholders, including policymakers, AI developers, educators, and community leaders, in order to address these challenges and ensure that the benefits of AI are equitably harnessed. By prioritizing fairness, transparency, and accountability in AI systems, investing in education and workforce development, addressing the digital divide, and advocating for privacy protections and ethical guidelines, we can create a more inclusive and equitable future for Black communities in the age of intelligent machines.

14

AI Ethics: Navigating the Societal Implications of Intelligent Machines

14.1 Introduction

As AI continues to permeate various aspects of our lives, it becomes increasingly important to address the ethical and societal implications of these technologies. This chapter explores the ethical landscape surrounding AI, focusing on new examples and information not previously mentioned in other chapters.

14.2 AI Ethics: Core Principles and Considerations

While we have touched on ethical principles such as transparency, fairness, privacy and data protection, accountability, and safety and security in previous chapters, it's important to highlight AI applications that have recently come under scrutiny for ethical concerns. For instance, AI-powered emotion recognition technology used in advertising or hiring processes can raise questions about consent, potential bias, and the accuracy of the algorithms.

AI-generated content, such as deepfakes, also poses significant ethical challenges. These realistic yet manipulated videos can be used for misinformation, harassment, and even political manipulation. The ethical principles of transparency and accountability are crucial when dealing with deepfake technology to ensure that users can differentiate between authentic and manipulated content.

Another emerging area of concern is the use of AI in the development of autonomous weapons systems. These systems, also known as "killer robots," have the potential to conduct warfare without direct human intervention. The ethical considerations surrounding such technology include the potential loss of human control, accountability, and the risk of escalation in armed conflicts. International efforts to regulate the development and deployment of autonomous weapons are essential in addressing these concerns.

14.3 AI and the Future of Work

In addition to the potential displacement of human workers, AI's impact on the future of work also includes ethical considerations related to worker autonomy and mental well-being.

As AI systems are increasingly used for decision-making in organizations, workers may experience a loss of autonomy and agency in their roles. It's essential to strike a balance between leveraging AI for productivity and preserving the human element in the workplace.

The use of AI in remote work environments also raises ethical concerns, particularly regarding employee privacy and mental well-being. AI-powered tools that track employee productivity and engagement can lead to excessive surveillance and invasion of privacy. Employers must balance the benefits of these technologies with the potential harm to employee well-being and trust.

Lastly, the ethics of AI systems used for talent acquisition and retention should be considered. AI algorithms used to screen job applicants and predict employee performance can introduce biases and lead to unfair treatment of certain demographics. It is crucial for organizations to monitor the fairness and transparency of these algorithms and ensure they align with the company's diversity and inclusion goals.

14.4 AI and Environmental Ethics

As AI's impact on society expands, it is essential to consider its implications on the environment and the ethical responsibilities that come with it.

AI can play a significant role in promoting sustainable development and addressing environmental challenges. For instance, AI-powered prediction models can be used to optimize renewable energy generation and consumption, improving the efficiency of solar and wind power systems. Moreover, AI-driven conservation initiatives can help monitor and protect endangered species by using machine learning algorithms to analyze data from cameras, drones, and satellite imagery, enabling conservationists to track animal populations and detect poaching activities.

However, AI's development and deployment also come with environmental costs. Training large-scale AI models requires significant computational resources and energy consumption, which can contribute to increased carbon emissions. Data centers powering AI systems are often associated with high energy usage, leading to concerns about their environmental impact.

AI for Climate Change Mitigation and Adaptation

AI has the potential to play a crucial role in addressing climate change by helping to reduce greenhouse gas emissions and supporting adaptation efforts. Some key applications include:

AI-powered climate models

Advanced machine learning techniques can be used to improve the accuracy and efficiency of climate models, enabling more precise predictions of future climate conditions and informing policy decisions.

Precision agriculture

AI-driven solutions can help farmers optimize their use of resources, such as water and fertilizers, leading to more sustainable agricultural practices and reduced environmental impact.

AI for Environmental Monitoring and Conservation

AI technologies can be leveraged to monitor and protect the environment more effectively. Some notable applications include:

Biodiversity monitoring

AI-powered image recognition algorithms can analyze data from cameras, drones, and satellites to identify and track plant and animal species, providing valuable information for conservation efforts.

Deforestation detection

AI algorithms can analyze satellite imagery to detect deforestation and land use changes, allowing for faster and more accurate identification of areas in need of intervention.

Pollution monitoring

AI systems can analyze air and water quality data, identifying pollution sources and helping to guide mitigation measures.

Environmental Impact of AI Development and Deployment

Despite the potential benefits of AI for environmental conservation and sustainability, there are also concerns about the environmental impact of AI development and deployment. Key issues include:

Energy consumption

Training large-scale AI models and running data centers require significant amounts of energy, which can contribute to increased carbon emissions. It is essential for the AI community to prioritize energy-efficient algorithms, hardware, and data center design to minimize the environmental footprint of AI systems.

Electronic waste

The rapid development and obsolescence of AI hardware can lead to increased electronic waste, with potentially negative consequences for the environment and human health. Responsible disposal and recycling of AI hardware, as well as exploring more sustainable materials and manufacturing processes, are essential for mitigating these impacts.

Ethical Considerations for AI and the Environment

To ensure that AI is developed and deployed in an environmentally responsible manner, several ethical considerations must be taken into account:

Transparency and accountability

Stakeholders must be informed about the environmental impact of AI systems and the efforts being made to minimize it. AI developers and operators should be held accountable for the environmental consequences of their systems.

Public engagement and participation

AI development and deployment for environmental purposes should involve public engagement, ensuring that the voices of affected communities are heard and their concerns addressed.

Interdisciplinary collaboration

Addressing the complex ethical and environmental challenges associated with AI requires collaboration among AI developers, environmental scientists, policymakers, and other stakeholders.

Sustainable AI development

AI researchers and developers should prioritize energy-efficient algorithms and hardware, minimizing the environmental impact of AI systems. In addition, exploring the use of renewable energy sources for data centers and other AI infrastructure can help reduce carbon emissions.

Responsible AI deployment

The use of AI in environmentally sensitive areas, such as wildlife habitats and protected ecosystems, should be approached with caution. AI applications in these contexts must be carefully designed and monitored to avoid unintended consequences, such as disruption of local flora and fauna.

Environmental justice

AI's role in environmental conservation should not disproportionately benefit certain populations or regions at the expense of others. Efforts to utilize AI for environmental purposes must be inclusive and equitable, ensuring that vulnerable communities and ecosystems receive adequate attention and resources.

Throughout this chapter, we have delved into the ethical considerations surrounding AI and explored various aspects of its societal impacts. By examining the importance of transparency, fairness, privacy, accountability, safety, and security, we have highlighted the need for a robust ethical framework to guide AI development and deployment. In doing

so, we have also touched upon the implications of AI for the
future of work and the environment.

15

Demystifying AI: Ensuring Meaningful Transparency and Redress for Harms

15.1 Introduction

The increasing prevalence of AI systems in our daily lives has brought about numerous benefits, as well as an array of potential harms. As AI continues to permeate various sectors of society, it becomes crucial to develop mechanisms that ensure transparency and redress for those who might be adversely affected by these technologies. In this chapter, we will explore the importance of transparency in AI systems and delve into the various ways in which individuals and communities can seek redress for harms caused by AI. By demystifying AI and understanding the mechanisms through which it operates, we can work towards creating a more equitable and inclusive digital landscape for everyone, including Black communities.

15.2 The Importance of Transparency in AI Systems

Transparency is a critical aspect of responsible AI development and deployment. Without a clear understanding of how AI systems operate and the basis on which they make decisions, it becomes difficult to hold these systems accountable and ensure their ethical use. A lack of transparency can lead to unintended consequences, such as the perpetuation of existing biases and the infringement of individuals' rights.

Transparency in AI systems encompasses several aspects

Algorithmic transparency

This refers to the comprehensibility and openness of the algorithms used in AI systems. It is essential for developers and users to understand the underlying logic and assumptions of these algorithms to ensure they are used responsibly and ethically.

Data transparency

AI systems rely on vast amounts of data for training and decision-making. Ensuring that the data used is representative of the intended user base and that its sources are transparent can help mitigate potential biases and ensure the fairness of AI systems.

Decision-making transparency

This involves understanding the factors and variables considered by AI systems when making decisions. It is crucial for users and stakeholders to comprehend the rationale behind AI-driven decisions, especially when these decisions have a significant impact on individuals' lives, such as in employment, healthcare, or criminal justice.

Governance and accountability transparency

AI systems must be developed, deployed, and managed in a transparent manner. This includes clearly defined processes for decision-making, oversight, and redress, as well as the disclosure of any potential conflicts of interest or ethical considerations.

15.3 Redress Mechanisms for AI Harms

In addition to ensuring transparency in AI systems, it is vital to establish mechanisms that allow individuals and communities to seek redress for any harms caused by AI technologies. These redress mechanisms can take various forms, including:

- Legal remedies: In cases where AI systems violate existing laws or regulations, affected individuals can pursue legal action to seek compensation or demand changes to the AI system in question. This may involve filing a lawsuit or lodging a complaint with the relevant regulatory body.

- Internal grievance mechanisms: Companies and organizations that develop or deploy AI systems should establish internal channels through which affected individuals can report any adverse impacts or concerns related to AI technologies. This may include the creation of dedicated complaint departments or the appointment of AI ethics officers.

- External oversight bodies: Governments and regulatory agencies can play a crucial role in ensuring redress for AI harms by establishing independent oversight bodies tasked with monitoring AI systems, conducting audits, and investigating complaints.

- Industry self-regulation: Companies and organizations involved in AI development can come together to establish industry-wide standards and guidelines aimed at minimizing harms and ensuring responsible AI practices. This may involve the creation of certification schemes, codes of conduct, or best practice guides.

- Public engagement and advocacy: Affected individuals and communities can raise awareness of AI-related harms and advocate for change by engaging with policymakers, industry leaders, and the wider public. This may involve organizing public campaigns, participating in consultations, or collaborating with civil society organizations to push for more robust AI regulations and redress mechanisms.

15.4 Challenges in Ensuring Transparency and Redress for AI Harms

While the need for transparency and redress in AI systems is widely recognized, there are several challenges that must be overcome to achieve meaningful progress in this area. Some of these challenges include:

- Technical complexity: AI algorithms, particularly those based on deep learning, can be highly complex and difficult to interpret. This can make it challenging for developers, users, and regulators to fully understand the inner workings of AI systems and assess their transparency.
- Trade-offs between transparency and performance: In some cases, achieving a high level of transparency in AI systems may come at the cost of reduced performance or efficiency. Striking the right balance between transparency and performance is essential to ensure the responsible deployment of AI technologies.
- Intellectual property concerns: Companies and organizations that develop AI systems may be reluctant to disclose proprietary information about their algorithms and data sources, making it challenging to ensure transparency and accountability.
- Inadequate legal and regulatory frameworks: Existing laws and regulations may not adequately address the unique

challenges posed by AI technologies, making it difficult for affected individuals to seek redress for AI-related harms.

- Limited awareness and understanding: Many individuals may not be fully aware of the potential harms associated with AI systems or the mechanisms available for seeking redress. This can make it challenging for those affected by AI technologies to effectively advocate for their rights and pursue remedies.

15.5 Addressing Challenges and Enhancing Transparency and Redress

To overcome the challenges associated with ensuring transparency and redress in AI systems, various strategies can be pursued, such as:

- Developing explainable AI techniques: Researchers and AI practitioners can work towards developing more interpretable and explainable AI models that provide a clearer understanding of their decision-making processes without sacrificing performance.
- Encouraging industry collaboration and standardization: Companies and organizations involved in AI development can collaborate to establish common standards, guidelines, and best practices aimed at promoting transparency and accountability.
- Strengthening legal and regulatory frameworks: Policymakers can work towards updating existing laws and

regulations to better address the unique challenges posed by AI technologies, ensuring that affected individuals have access to effective redress mechanisms.

- Raising awareness and empowering individuals: Efforts should be made to educate individuals and communities about the potential harms associated with AI systems and the mechanisms available for seeking redress. This may involve public education campaigns, workshops, and collaborations with civil society organizations.
- Encouraging public participation and engagement: Policymakers and AI developers can involve the public in the development, deployment, and oversight of AI technologies, ensuring that the perspectives of affected individuals and communities are taken into account.

In this chapter, we have explored the importance of transparency and redress in AI systems, particularly for Black communities. We have discussed the challenges that must be overcome in ensuring meaningful transparency and redress, including technical complexity, trade-offs between transparency and performance, intellectual property concerns, inadequate legal and regulatory frameworks, and limited awareness and understanding. To address these challenges, we have highlighted strategies such as developing explainable AI techniques, encouraging industry collaboration and standardization, strengthening legal and regulatory frameworks, raising awareness and empowering individuals, and encouraging public participation and engagement. By demystifying AI and working towards these goals, we can contribute to a more equitable and inclusive digital landscape, ensuring that the benefits of AI technologies are enjoyed by all while minimizing potential drawbacks and risks.

16

Building an Equitable Future: Championing Inclusivity and Justice in AI

16.1 Envisioning an Equitable Future with AI

In an equitable future with AI, the benefits and opportunities afforded by these technologies would be accessible to all, regardless of race, ethnicity, or socioeconomic background. To paint a picture of what such a future might look like, let's delve into some key aspects that expand on the ideas previously discussed in this book.

Diverse perspectives in AI system evaluation

Building on the notion of inclusive AI development from earlier chapters, AI systems would be evaluated by diverse panels of experts and community representatives. This would ensure that different viewpoints are considered, leading to AI technologies that are better suited to address the unique needs and challenges faced by various communities, including Black communities.

Ethical AI impact assessments

Beyond transparent and accountable AI systems mentioned earlier, organizations would conduct comprehensive ethical AI impact assessments before deploying AI technologies. These assessments would consider potential harms and benefits for all stakeholders, helping to identify and mitigate risks and ensuring that AI systems promote fairness and equity.

Equitable distribution of AI-generated wealth

In an equitable future, the wealth generated by AI technologies would be distributed fairly across society, reducing income inequality and creating opportunities for marginalized communities. Policies and regulations could be established to ensure that the economic benefits of AI-driven innovations are shared more broadly.

AI-enabled capacity-building in marginalized communities

AI technologies would be used to support capacity-building initiatives in marginalized communities, such as mentorship programs, skill development workshops, and resource-sharing platforms. By leveraging AI to create opportunities for growth and empowerment, we can work towards closing social and economic gaps.

Digital rights advocacy and education

In addition to robust legal and regulatory frameworks, organizations and community leaders would engage in digital rights advocacy and education efforts. This would involve raising awareness about AI-related rights and providing resources to help individuals navigate the complex landscape of AI technologies, ensuring that they are equipped to participate in the digital world.

Collaborative AI research and development

Researchers, developers, and stakeholders from various sectors would come together to engage in collaborative AI research and development projects. These collaborative efforts would focus on addressing the specific needs and challenges faced by marginalized communities, fostering innovative solutions that promote equity and inclusion.

16.2 Final Thoughts

Throughout this book, we have explored various aspects of AI and its implications for Black communities. From understanding the basics of AI technology to analyzing its potential benefits and challenges, we have sought to provide a comprehensive overview of the current state of AI and its impact on society.

As we've discussed earlier, AI has the potential to revolutionize numerous sectors, including healthcare, education, and criminal justice. These advancements can lead to improved outcomes and increased opportunities for Black communities. However, we must also be cognizant of the potential risks associated with AI technologies, such as biases, lack of transparency, and limited access to resources.

To mitigate these risks and ensure equitable AI development and deployment, we've highlighted the importance of representation and diversity in the field of AI, as well as the need for public engagement and advocacy. We have also emphasized the significance of transparency in AI systems and establishing redress mechanisms for those adversely affected by AI technologies.

As AI continues to evolve and permeate our daily lives, it is crucial for individuals, communities, organizations, and governments to remain vigilant and actively work towards creating a more inclusive and just digital landscape. By fostering collaboration among stakeholders, promoting responsible AI practices, and advocating for the rights of marginalized communities, we can harness the potential of AI to improve the lives of Black communities and beyond.

In closing, I hope that this book has provided valuable insights and stimulated thought and discussion on the role of AI in shaping the future of Black communities. By coming together to address the challenges and seize the opportunities presented by AI, we can work towards a brighter and more equitable future for all.

17

Afterword

Thriving as Black Individuals in the Era of AI

Thriving in this new era requires a multifaceted approach, encompassing education, community engagement, advocacy, and a continuous pursuit of digital equity. The knowledge gained from this book is a powerful foundation, but it must be supplemented with real-world information, tools, and resources to create advantageous situations and foster personal and collective success.

The goal is not merely to survive but to thrive and empower Black individuals in the AI era. This comprehensive roadmap provides easy-to-apply information and resources, guiding you from the very beginning to a point of mastery and success.

Step 1: Develop a Strong Foundation in Digital Literacy

Before diving into AI-specific skills, it is essential to build a strong foundation in digital literacy. Familiarize yourself with basic computer skills, online research techniques, and tools for digital collaboration and communication.

Resource: Northstar Digital Literacy offers free online assessments and learning resources to help you build essential digital skills.

Step 2: Explore AI and Its Applications

Develop a general understanding of AI and its applications across industries. This will help you identify areas where your interests and AI intersect.

Resource: "AI For Everyone", a free online course from Coursera, provides a non-technical introduction to AI and its potential impact on society.

Step 3: Acquire Technical Skills

Once you have a basic understanding of AI, focus on acquiring technical skills relevant to your interests. Learn programming languages like Python or R, which are commonly used in AI and data science. Explore machine learning concepts, data analysis techniques, and visualization tools.

Resource: Codecademyoffers interactive coding courses in Python, R, and other programming languages, while Google's Machine Learning Crash Course provides a comprehensive introduction to machine learning.

Step 4: Deepen Your AI Knowledge

After acquiring basic technical skills, delve deeper into AI and machine learning concepts. Learn about neural networks, natural language processing, computer vision, and reinforcement learning. Understand the ethical implications and challenges associated with AI, such as fairness, accountability, transparency, and privacy.

Resource: Fast.ai offers free, in-depth courses on deep learning and AI, while OpenAI provides numerous resources and research papers on AI ethics and safety.

Step 5: Engage with the AI Community

Connect with other AI enthusiasts and professionals to share knowledge, collaborate, and stay up-to-date on the latest developments in the field. Attend meetups, conferences, and workshops, and participate in online forums and discussions.

Resource: AI Meetups lists AI-related events happening around the world, while AI Stack Exchange is an online Q&A platform where you can ask and answer AI-related questions.

Step 6: Gain Practical Experience

Apply your AI knowledge and skills to real-world projects. This can be through internships, freelance work, or personal projects. Developing a portfolio of practical AI experience will increase your employability and credibility in the field.

Resource: Kaggle offers a platform for data science competitions and collaboration, where you can work on real-world problems and learn from others in the community.

Step 7: Advocate for Digital Equity and Ethical AI

As you advance in the AI field, use your knowledge and influence to advocate for digital equity and ethical AI. Support policies and initiatives that address the digital divide and digital redlining, and hold tech companies accountable for creating fair, transparent, and unbiased AI systems.

Resource: The AI Now Institute conducts research and advocacy focused on the social implications of AI, providing valuable resources and insights to support your advocacy efforts.

Step 8: Mentor and Inspire Others

As you grow in your AI journey, give back to your community by mentoring and inspiring others. Share your knowledge, experiences, and resources with those who are just starting their AI journey. By doing so, you contribute to the development of a more diverse and inclusive AI ecosystem.

Resource: Black in AI is a community that promotes diversity in the AI field. They offer mentorship, networking opportunities, and resources for Black individuals interested in AI.

Step 9: Pursue Career Opportunities in AI

Leverage your AI knowledge, skills, and experience to pursue rewarding career opportunities across various industries. Whether you choose to work in research, product development, or consulting, your expertise in AI can help you make a positive impact in the world.

Resource: LinkedIn is a valuable platform for job searching and networking in the AI field. You can find job listings, connect with professionals, and join AI-related groups to stay informed about industry trends.

Step 10: Continue Learning and Adapting

AI is a rapidly evolving field, and staying current with the latest advancements is crucial for success. Regularly update your skills, attend workshops and conferences, and embrace a lifelong learning mindset. By doing so, you'll ensure that you remain at the forefront of AI innovation.

Resource: arXiv is a free online repository of research papers in various scientific domains, including AI. Regularly reviewing publications in your area of interest can help you stay up-to-date with the latest advancements.

Let's reflect on the broader perspectives and strategies that can contribute to thriving as a Black individual in the AI era, beyond the roadmap we've provided.

Embrace a Growth Mindset

Cultivate a growth mindset, which emphasizes the belief that intelligence and abilities can be developed through effort and learning. This mindset can help you overcome challenges, learn from mistakes, and continuously improve your skills and knowledge in the AI field.

Celebrate and Leverage Your Unique Perspective

As a Black individual in the AI field, you bring a unique perspective that is valuable for developing inclusive and equitable AI solutions. Embrace your identity and experiences, and use them to contribute meaningfully to the development and application of AI technologies.

Stay Informed About AI Policies and Regulations

Keep track of local, national, and international policies and regulations related to AI, as these can have a significant impact on your work and career opportunities. Being well-versed in AI policy will also help you advocate for ethical and inclusive AI development.

Seek Interdisciplinary Collaborations

AI can benefit from the integration of diverse disciplines, such as psychology, sociology, and ethics. Pursue interdisciplinary collaborations to expand your understanding of AI's societal impact and develop more effective, human-centered AI solutions.

Focus on Self-Care and Mental Health

Thriving in the AI era goes beyond professional success. Prioritize self-care and mental health to maintain a balanced and fulfilling life. Engage in activities that promote relaxation, mindfulness, and physical well-being.

Thriving as a Black individual in the AI era is achievable by following a systematic roadmap, acquiring relevant skills, engaging with the AI community, and advocating for digital equity and ethical AI. By using the knowledge, tools, and resources shared in this book, you can create advantageous situations and make a lasting impact in the world of AI.

18

NOTES

Chapter 10 Footnotes

[1] DeepMind - AlphaFold: https://deepmind.com/research/case-studies/alphafold

[2] Esteva, A., Kuprel, B., Novoa, R. A., Ko, J., Swetter, S. M., Blau, H. M., & Thrun, S. (2017). Dermatologist-level classification of skin cancer with deep neural networks. Nature, 542(7639), 115–118. https://doi.org/10.1038/nature21056

[3] Zebra Medical Vision: https://www.zebra-med.com/

[4] Zest AI: https://www.zest.ai/

[5] Bartlett, R. P., Morse, A., Stanton, R., & Wallace, N. (2019). Consumer Lending Discrimination in the FinTech Era. NBER Working Paper No. 25943. https://www.nber.org/papers/w2

5943

[6] Fagnant, D. J., & Kockelman, K. (2015). Preparing a nation for autonomous vehicles: Opportunities, barriers and policy recommendations. Transportation Research Part A: Policy and Practice, 77, 167–181. https://doi.org/10.1016/j.tra.2015.04.003

[7] Wilson, B., Hoffman, J., & Morgenstern, J. (2019). Predictive Inequity in Object Detection. In Proceedings of the IEEE/CVF Conference on Computer Vision and Pattern Recognition (CVPR).

[8] Carnegie Learning - MATHia: https://www.carnegielearning.com/products/software-platform/mathia/

[9] Thinkster Math: https://hellothinkster.com/

Chapter 11 Footnotes

[10] Buolamwini, J., & Gebru, T. (2018). Gender Shades: Intersectional Accuracy Disparities in Commercial Gender Classification. Proceedings of Machine Learning Research, 81, 1-15.

[11] Snow, J. (2018). Amazon's Face Recognition Falsely Matched 28 Members of Congress With Mugshots. ACLU.

[12] Lum, K., & Isaac, W. (2016). To predict and serve?

Significance, 13(5), 14-19.

[13] Angwin, J., Larson, J., Mattu, S., & Kirchner, L. (2016).
Machine Bias. ProPublica. https://www.propublica.org/articl
e/machine-bias-risk-assessments-in-criminal-sentencing

[14] Reuters: https://www.reuters.com/article/us-amazon-co
m-jobs-automation-insight/amazon-scraps-secret-ai-recruiti
ng-tool-that-showed-bias-against-women-idUSKCN1MK08
G

[15] Ali, M., Sapiezynski, P., Bogen, M., Korolova, A., Mislove,
A., & Rieke, A. (2019). Discrimination through optimization:
How Facebook's ad delivery can lead to skewed outcomes.
ACM Conference on Computer-Supported Cooperative Work
and Social Computing (CSCW).

[16] Sweeney, L. (2013). Discrimination in online ad delivery.
Communications of the ACM, 56(5), 44–54.

[17] Obermeyer, Z., Powers, B., Vogeli, C., & Mullainathan, S.
(2019). Dissecting racial bias in an algorithm used to manage
the health of populations. Science, 366(6464), 447–453.

Chapter 12 Footnotes

[18] Telecommunications Act of 1996, Pub. L. No. 104-104,
110 Stat. 56 (1996). https://www.congress.gov/104/plaws/pu
bl104/PLAW-104publ104.pdf

[19] One Laptop per Child (OLPC). (2005). One Laptop per Child: Our Mission. http://one.laptop.org/about/mission

[20] Federal Communications Commission. (2010). Connecting America: The National Broadband Plan. https://www.fcc.gov/national-broadband-plan

[21] The White House, President Barack Obama. (2013). ConnectED: President Obama's Plan for Connecting All Schools to the Digital Age. https://obamawhitehouse.archives.gov/issues/education/k-12/connected

[22] National Digital Inclusion Alliance. (n.d.). Digital Inclusion Trailblazers. https://www.digitalinclusion.org/trailblazers/

[23] EveryoneOn. (n.d.). About Us. https://www.everyoneon.org/about

[24] The Digital Equity Laboratory. (n.d.). About the Digital Equity Laboratory. https://www.digitalequitylab.org/about

[25] Federal Communications Commission. (n.d.). Lifeline Support for Affordable Communications. https://www.fcc.gov/general/lifeline-program-low-income-consumers

[26] Federal Communications Commission. (n.d.). Schools and Libraries (E-Rate). https://www.fcc.gov/general/schools-and-libraries-e-rate

[27] American Rescue Plan Act of 2021, Pub. L. No. 117-2, 135 Stat. 4 (2021). https://www.congress.gov/117/plaws/publ2/P

LAW-117publ2.pdf

[28] State of California. (n.d.). California Broadband Council.
https://broadbandcouncil.ca.gov/

[29] Microsoft. (n.d.). Microsoft Airband Initiative. https://w
ww.microsoft.com/en-us/airband